LIFE IN THE NEW TESTAMENT WORLD

Understanding Professions,
Practices, and Politics

Armin J. Panning

Northwestern Publishing House
Milwaukee, Wisconsin

Cover illustrations: Lars Justinen; GoodSalt, Inc.
Art Director: Karen Knutson
Designer: Pamela Dunn

Scripture is taken from the HOLY BIBLE, NEW INTERNATIONAL VERSION®. NIV®. Copyright © 1973, 1978, 1984 by Biblica, Inc.™ Used by permission of Zondervan. All rights reserved worldwide.

All rights reserved. This publication may not be copied, photocopied, reproduced, translated, or converted to any electronic or machine-readable form in whole or in part, except for brief quotations, without prior written approval from the publisher.

Northwestern Publishing House
1250 N. 113th St., Milwaukee, WI 53226-3284
www.nph.net
© 2011 by Northwestern Publishing House
Published 2011
Printed in the United States of America
ISBN 978-8100-2373-4

Table of Contents

Preface 5

One
Gainful Employment 7
    Farming 7
    Growing Grapes 9
    Growing Olives 12
    Harvesting 14
    Threshing 15
    Growing Figs 18
    Mustard 21
    Fishing 22
    Fish 29
    Publishing 32
    Lawyers and Teachers of the Law 36
    Teaching 39
    Construction Trades 45
    Tent Making 48

Two
Commerce and Trade 50
    Barter 50
    Large Sums 53
    Small Coins 55
    Value-Neutral Coins 56

Three
Travel and Transport 62
    Travel on Foot 62
    Riding 65
    Roads 66
    Travel by Water 70

Four
The Roman Occupation of Palestine:
A Sketch of Roman History 83

Introduction 83
Founding of the City 83
The Roman Monarchy 84
The Roman Republic 85
The Roman Empire 91
Subjugation and Occupation of Palestine 93
Roman Provinces.............................. 94
Provincial Administration.................... 95
The Roman Legal System 109
Roman Citizenship 115
Roman Census................................. 117
Roman Taxes 118

FIVE
Jewish Puppet Government..................... 120
    Sadducees and Pharisees.................. 120
    The Sanhedrin 120
    Petty Kings 121
    The Herodians 122

SIX
Christian Interaction With New Testament Society........... 130
    Orthodox Jewish Community 130
    Interaction With Roman Government:
    Christianity as a "Legal Religion" 132
    Emperor Worship 133

BIBLIOGRAPHY 135

INDEX 136

Preface

In keeping with the general intent of the Bible Discovery series, this volume is a nontechnical treatment intended for the average Bible reader. It is intended to help the reader understand life in New Testament times. It is neither comprehensive nor exhaustive, but rather a collection of items, loosely arranged by subject. Basically it aims to reflect conditions in the Greco-Roman world of the first century A.D. Hopefully increased insight into these matters—cultural, political, geographical—will enhance your reading of God's Word and increase your understanding and appreciation of how God ordered all things so as to bring about the impressive growth and extension of the early Christian church. Or to use our Savior's picture, we see glimpses of the "mustard plant" extending its branches into the entire then-known world.

Gainful Employment

Farming

Even a casual reading of Scripture shows that New Testament people gained their livelihoods in various ways. Despite that diversity, it's safe to say that in general people of that time lived closer to the land than most of us do today. Israel was largely an agricultural society. People themselves were engaged in growing their own food or could easily observe those doing so. Hence, without any fear of losing his readers, James could say:

> Be patient, then, brothers, until the Lord's coming. See how the farmer waits for the land to yield its valuable crop and how patient he is for the autumn and spring rains. You too, be patient and stand firm, because the Lord's coming is near. (James 5:7,8)

We of the 21st century, often in our urban settings, don't "see" the farmer. Hence, we may need a bit of help to grasp the connection between the Jewish farmer's need for patience in awaiting a crop and the Christian's need for patience in coping with spiritual matters. It will help if we understand the Mediterranean climate with which the farmer of James' day had to cope.

During the four hottest months of the year (June to September), it is virtually certain that Palestine will receive no rain at all. The soil becomes bone-dry and baked hard, leaving no chance for preparing the soil. Softening the soil so that it can be worked up and seeded happens when the "autumn . . . rains" (literally, the "*early . . . rains*") begin to fall in October or November. Their arrival is erratic but eagerly sought by the farmer.

The winter months (December to February) are the wettest times of the year and bring most of Palestine's modest rainfall. The long-term average in Jerusalem, for example, is 26 inches annually, with a maximum of 40 inches and a minimum of 12 inches. Winter is the main growing season. But very important for the heads of grain to fill out properly are the "spring rains" (literally, the "*latter* rains") that are expected in April and May. These are essential for determining whether it will be a bumper crop, an average crop, or perhaps only a very limited one.

The farmer is dependent on the annual rainfall. He cannot control it, but he is confident that it will come. James is urging his readers not to become discouraged. Everything will be set right at the proper time. The farmer may not know *when* the rain is coming, but he is confident *that it will* come. Also for us, the present is often dark and the future unknown, but by pointing us to the example of the Jewish farmer, James directs us to God's promises and urges us, "You too, be patient and stand firm, because the Lord's coming is near" (James 5:8).

Living close to the land often gave rural people an advantage in catching the point of the agricultural illustrations Jesus was fond of using in his teaching. Still, those who are acquainted with the marvelous farmland the Lord has provided in the broad heartlands of the U.S. may have trouble with a parable such as the one Jesus told about a sower sowing seed on four kinds of soil:

> *Then [Jesus] told them many things in parables, saying: "A farmer went out to sow his seed. As he was scattering the seed, some fell along the path, and the birds came and ate it up. Some fell on rocky places, where it did not have much soil. It sprang up quickly, because the soil was shallow. But when the sun came up, the plants were scorched, and they withered because they had no root. Other seed fell among thorns, which grew up and choked the plants. Still other seed fell on good soil, where it produced a crop—a hundred, sixty or thirty times what was sown. He who has ears, let him hear."* (Matthew 13:3-9)

It would be a mistake to think here of large, rectangular grain fields or long, straight lines of row crops. Except for a few instances of such fields in the gently sloping valleys of Galilee, there are no large, geometric fields in Palestine. Small, irregular patches of tillable soil grubbed out between rocky outcroppings are the norm. Even today, using field machinery is largely impractical. Farmers still go out and scatter seed by hand, much as we might do to fix bare patches in our lawn. Obviously, this is not a precise operation.

If the tillable patches are separated by where people walk, there will be a path through the field. Some of the scattered seed will fall on the path, to be immediately "harvested" by the birds. Other seed that falls on the thin top soil covering the underlying rock will sprout quickly but just as quickly get burned up by the blazing Mediterranean sun. And thorns and thistles have been the farmer's nemesis ever since the fall into sin. Fortunately, however, there is also the deep soil that produces a bountiful crop.

Even if we don't have the same conditions in our backyards, if we understand Jesus' picture, the parable makes perfect sense for illustrating the truth that Jesus himself indicates as the point of his lesson. In Matthew 13:18-23 Jesus informs his disciples, and us, that the "seed" is the Word and that the four kinds of "soil" illustrate the response (or lack of response) the Word receives in human hearts. Jesus graphically illustrates the situation and adds the sober warning, "He who has ears, let him hear." What Jesus taught in picture language, the writer to the Hebrews repeats in literal form, citing Psalm 95, "Today, if you hear his voice, do not harden your hearts" (Hebrews 3:7,8).

Growing Grapes

It would be hard to overestimate the important role wine played in the lives of Jewish people living in New Testament times. Wine had a religious function, being used as a drink offering with some of the Levitical sacrifices. It was used to celebrate festive occasions. Recall the water Jesus turned into wine at the wedding in Cana. "Wine that gladdens the heart" (Psalm 104:15) was used also on sad occasions, for example, to cheer mourners. It was assumed to have antiseptic qualities, which is how it was used by the good Samarian who poured wine into the wounds of the traveler mugged on his way to Jericho (Luke 10:30-37). Paul attests to wine's medicinal qualities when he urges its moderate use to remedy a stomach problem that afflicted Timothy (1 Timothy 5:23).

But by far wine's most prominent feature was its daily use at the dining table. Even if families didn't have their own grape arbors, they would certainly be acquainted with the large, commercial operations that flourished in Palestine, whose soil and climate is so well suited for growing grapevines.

These larger commercial operations serve as the basis for Jesus' parable, teaching an important lesson to people who were rejecting John the Baptist's call to "look, the Lamb of God" (John 1:29). Jesus said:

> *"John came to you to show you the way of righteousness, and you did not believe him, but the tax collectors and the prostitutes did. And even after you saw this, you did not repent and believe him.*
>
> *"Listen to another parable: There was a landowner who planted a vineyard. He put a wall around it, dug a winepress in it and built a watchtower. Then he rented the vineyard to some farmers and went away on a journey. When the harvest time approached, he sent his servants to the tenants to collect his fruit.*
>
> *"The tenants seized his servants; they beat one, killed another, and stoned a third. Then he sent other servants to them, more than the first time, and the tenants treated them the same way. Last of all, he sent his son to them. 'They will respect my son,' he said.*
>
> *"But when the tenants saw the son, they said to each other, 'This is the heir. Come, let's kill him and take his inheritance.' So they took him and threw him out of the vineyard and killed him.*
>
> *"Therefore, when the owner of the vineyard comes, what will he do to those tenants?"*
>
> *"He will bring those wretches to a wretched end," they replied, "and he will rent the vineyard to other tenants, who will give him his share of the crop at harvest time."* (Matthew 21:32-41)

The landowner who planted the vineyard took all the necessary precautions to protect his investment. He built a wall around it to keep out predators and thieves. He even added a security system by building a watchtower. But the centerpiece of the project was the winepress. Forget about any kind of hydraulic system to press the grapes. The New Testament winepress consisted of a pit into which barefooted workers descended and trampled the clusters of ripe grapes. The extracted juice flowed into adjoining catch basins from which the liquid could be dipped for filtering and fermenting into wine.

Just how big were such winepresses? Obviously they varied in size, but one example may be of interest and serve as an illustration. A number of years ago, Wisconsin Lutheran Seminary entered into an arrangement to cooperate with the University of Tel Aviv on a five-week "dig" at a *tel* (a mound indicating the presence of an ancient city) outside of Tel Aviv. That expedition uncovered what at the time was described as the second-largest winepress to have been excavated in modern Israel. The floor of the pit where the grapes were trampled measured 5 meters by 5 meters (16' x 16'), with two somewhat smaller holding tanks, or settling basins, next to it.

Almost always, parables contain some elements that are merely the framework of the story. As such they are not essential for understanding the lesson being taught in the parable. Here the size of the winepress is not important. Rather, it is the press' centrality to the operation and its value to both the owner and tenants that is the focus of our attention.

The winepress signals the fact that something very important is at stake here. In fact, it involves the eternal fate of the hearers of the parable. The owner (God the Father) has prepared his plan of salvation, but the tenants (the Jewish nation) have not only rejected the commissioned servants (the prophets and Jesus' forerunner, John), but they even have designs on killing the Son (Christ).

The parable issues an earnest warning to those who reject God's salvation in Christ. Even Christ's enemies who heard the parable had to admit: Such people will come to a "wretched end." But the parable also extends a glorious ray of hope, as Jesus' enemies inadvertently taught in their answer: ". . . and he will rent the vineyard to other tenants."

Who are those "other tenants"? They are the same people the Good Shepherd speaks of when, using a different picture, he says, "I have other sheep that are not of this sheep pen. I must bring them also" (John 10:16). Obviously he is speaking of the inclusion of Gentiles into the New Testament church, which is consistent with God's plan from the beginning as spelled out in his promise to Abraham: Through his offspring, *all* the nations of the earth would be blessed.

Growing Olives

The apostle Paul devoted a major section of his letter to the Romans (chapters 9–11) to the relationship of Gentiles to Jews in the Christian church. To illustrate that relationship, he used another picture from the plant world, olive trees.

In the early days of the New Testament, the Christian church rapidly became identified with the Gentile community. Hence, in writing to the Romans, Paul had to warn the Gentiles against a serious misunderstanding. Gentiles were inclined to think God had rejected the Jews, his original chosen nation, and had replaced them with the Gentiles as the sole object of his affection. Paul had to warn them, "Do not boast over those [Jewish] branches. . . . Do not be arrogant, but be afraid" (Romans 11:20).

The apostle compared his Gentile readers to branches grafted into an olive tree. He wrote:

I am talking to you Gentiles. Inasmuch as I am the apostle to the Gentiles, I make much of my ministry in the hope that I may somehow arouse my own people to envy and save some of them.

If some of the branches have been broken off, and you [Gentiles], though a wild olive shoot, have been grafted in among the others and now share in the nourishing sap from the olive root, do not boast over those branches. If you do, consider this: You do not support the root, but the root supports you.

Consider therefore the kindness and sternness of God: sternness to those who fell, but kindness to you, provided that you continue in his kindness. Otherwise, you also will be cut off.

After all, if you [Gentiles] were cut out of an olive tree that is wild by nature, and contrary to nature were grafted into a cultivated olive tree, how much more readily will these, the natural branches [the Jews], be grafted into their own olive tree! (Romans 11:13, 14,17,18,22,24)

Perhaps you have seen an apple tree with five or more varieties of luscious apples hanging from its branches. We might think of the practice of grafting as a modern horticultural advancement. Actually, grafting has been practiced for thousands of years. That's why Paul used it to illustrate the relationship of Jews and Gentiles over against God's plan of salvation.

In principle, grafting is a rather simple process. A branch from a tree bearing good fruit (the *tame*, or domesticated, branch) is carefully cut and fitted to a branch of a tree that's main virtue is having a hardy root system (the *wild* root system). The trick is to keep the two parts together until the nourishing sap of the root fuses the two branches together and the wild root system supports the tame branch.

In the case of the Gentiles being grafted into the Jewish rootstock through the preaching of the gospel, God abandoned the normal grafting procedure. This was done in a way "contrary to nature." When most of God's chosen nation, Israel, rejected his plan of salvation through faith in Christ, it would have been logical for God to look for *good* people to graft into the Jews' fruitless rootstock. But he chose wild branches, the Gentiles, who of themselves added nothing good to the vine. Lest the Gentiles become proud as the Jews had, Paul reminded them that whatever fruit they bore came from the Jewish rootstock, specifically, the root of the Jewish Messiah. Recall Jesus' statement to the Samaritan woman at Jacob's well, "Salvation is from the Jews" (John 4:22). Gentiles have nothing to boast of and no grounds on which to lord it over the Jews. On the other hand, the Jews, through the Messiah, support the Gentiles and enable them to produce good fruit.

Still today, the Christian church is largely a Gentile entity. Most of us are Gentiles. Paul's illustration, drawn from the olive orchard, serves as a useful reminder of God's grace and mercy to us.

However, our inclusion in the Christian church is a favored position not only to cherish but also to share. It is easy to dismiss evangelism to Jews as a questionable use of our time and resources. We need to be reminded of Paul's assessment of the situation. He wrote: "If they [Jews] do not persist in unbelief, they will be grafted in, for God is able to graft them in again. After all, if you [Gentiles] were cut out of an olive tree that is wild by nature, and contrary to nature were grafted into a cultivated olive tree, how much more readily will these, the natural branches, be grafted into their own olive tree!" (Romans 11:23,24).

God has not given up on the Jewish nation. Neither should we.

Harvesting

If our idea of grain harvesting is limited to the picture of a large, self-propelled combine simultaneously cutting and threshing wide swaths of standing grain, then we are ill-equipped to understand the decidedly low-tech methods Jesus assumes in his harvest parables. Actually, such low-tech methods were employed well into the early days of our own country.

There are artists' depictions of early settlers using handheld, curved sickles, or "reaping hooks." The harvester had to cut and gather the grain stalks into neat little stacks that could be tied into bundles by a follow-up crew. Contemporary estimates suggest that by this method, harvesters could cut about three quarters of an acre per day.

Productivity increased when a long handle was attached to the blade, thus creating a scythe. A significant improvement resulted from adding a "cradle" to the scythe in order to catch the cut stalks. With a flip of the handle, the harvester could lay out an appropriate number of stalks for hand tying into bundles. This improvement increased productivity to an estimated four or five acres per day.

A significant upgrade occurred when in 1834 Cyrus McCormick introduced his horse-drawn reaper. The device was basically a hay mower equipped with a paddle wheel to tip the cut stalks back onto a platform. From this platform a worker, walking alongside the machine, could pull off the right number of stalks for tying into bundles.

But the main improvement to the reaper came when it was outfitted with a device that could also tie the cut stalks into bundles. After some ill-fated attempts to tie the bundles with wire, John F. Appleby of Mazomanie, Wisconsin, devised the first successful twine binder. Eventually Cyrus McCormick bought the rights to use the new improvement on his reapers, and the modern era of grain harvesting was launched.

The first harvest parable to engage our attention has Jesus assuming the very lowest level of technology. The weeds, and also the wheat, are pulled by hand. Note that Jesus assumes both the weeds and the wheat are hand tied:

Gainful Employment

> Jesus told them another parable: "The kingdom of heaven is like a man who sowed good seed in his field. But while everyone was sleeping, his enemy came and sowed weeds among the wheat, and went away. When the wheat sprouted and formed heads, then the weeds also appeared.
>
> "The owner's servants came to him and said, 'Sir, didn't you sow good seed in your field? Where then did the weeds come from?'
>
> "'An enemy did this,' he replied.
>
> "The servants asked him, 'Do you want us to go and pull them up?'
>
> "'No,' he answered, 'because while you are pulling the weeds, you may root up the wheat with them. Let both grow together until the harvest. At that time I will tell the harvesters: First collect the weeds and tie them in bundles to be burned; then gather the wheat and bring it into my barn.'" (Matthew 13:24-30)

In a second harvest parable, Jesus specifically mentions cutting with a sickle:

> He also said, "This is what the kingdom of God is like. A man scatters seed on the ground. Night and day, whether he sleeps or gets up, the seed sprouts and grows, though he does not know how. All by itself the soil produces grain—first the stalk, then the head, then the full kernel in the head. As soon as the grain is ripe, he puts the sickle to it, because the harvest has come." (Mark 4:26-29)

Incidentally, notice the three stages of growth Jesus assumes his listeners will be acquainted with. He speaks of "stalk," "head," and "full kernel." These stages of growth are in response to the three stages of the rainy season discussed in connection with James 5:7,8. The early rains (autumn) allow the sowing and sprouting of the seed. The main growing season during the winter rains produces the headed stalk, while the latter rains (spring) are very important in producing the "full kernel in the head."

Threshing

In his parable of weeds infiltrating a wheat field, Jesus teaches us that even though there will always be wicked people in the world, there will also be those who remain faithful to their Lord. The latter are pictured as bundles of grain brought in by the harvesters.

Although Jesus doesn't specifically include it in his parable of the weeds and the wheat, his listeners knew that the wheat needed somehow to be removed from the heads of the bundled stalks. The wheat had to be threshed before the kernels could be stored.

This is what is happening in the following prophecy of Isaiah:

> Listen and hear my voice; pay attention and hear what I say. When a farmer plows for planting, does he plow continually? Does he keep on breaking up and harrowing the soil? When he has leveled the surface, does he not sow caraway and scatter cummin? Does he not plant wheat in its place, barley in its plot, and spelt in its field? His God instructs him and teaches him the right way.
>
> Caraway is not threshed with a sledge, nor is a cartwheel rolled over cummin; caraway is beaten out with a rod, and cummin with a stick. Grain must be ground to make bread; so one does not go on threshing it forever. Though he drives the wheels of his threshing cart over it, his horses do not grind it. (Isaiah 28:23-28)

The farmer works to produce a crop in an orderly way. He threshes the seeds and grain in ways appropriate to them. So the Lord works in an orderly way to accomplish his salvation and work in the hearts of his people.

In this illustration Isaiah describes two kinds of harvesting. First Isaiah speaks of harvesting herb seeds grown in the home garden. Intended as flavoring for foods rather than the entrée itself, they were grown in small quantities and harvested in a special way. As described here, a harvester would take a handful of ripe stalks and beat them with a stick, catching the dislodged seeds on a cloth or in a basket.

But there is another kind of harvesting that Isaiah refers to, and this is also the kind of harvesting Jesus refers to in his harvest parables. This is the harvesting of field grains such as wheat, barley, or spelt (a low-grade wheat).

A major requirement for grain harvesting is a threshing floor. These can still be found in modern Israel, little changed from Jesus' or even Isaiah's time. A modern commentator describes the ancient threshing floor as follows: "A level, circular area twenty-five to forty feet in diameter, it was constructed in or near the grain field, preferably on an elevated spot exposed to the wind. It was prepared by removing the loose stones (by which a grain-containing border was made), then wetting and tamping the ground, and finally sweeping it" (G. B. Funderburk, *Zondervan Pictorial Encyclopedia of the Bible*, see "threshing floor").

Once the threshing floor was built, there had to be a way of removing the ripened kernels from the heads of the stalks. There were two main ways to do this. The first was the trampling method. Both the Hebrew and the Greek words for *threshing* have a root meaning "to tread on" or "to trample." This is a clear reference to the trampling method of threshing God was referring to in Deuteronomy 25:4, "Do not muzzle an ox while it is treading out the grain." Paul twice (I Corinthians 9:9; I Timothy 5:17,18) uses that Old Testament picture to make his point that just as an ox treading out grain should not be prohibited from helping himself to some of the grain he is harvesting, so also the one who brings people the gospel should not be deprived of support from that gospel.

In the verse we quoted from Isaiah previously, however, Isaiah has another method of threshing in mind. He speaks of threshing using either of two types of mechanical aid: a sledge or a cart. Isaiah says:

> *Caraway is not threshed with a* sledge, *nor is a* cartwheel *rolled over cummin; caraway is beaten out with a rod, and cummin with a stick. Grain must be ground to make bread; so one does not go on threshing it forever. Though he drives the wheels of his threshing cart over it, his horses do not grind it.* (Isaiah 28:27,28)

The main difference between these two harvesting devices seems to be the presence or absence of wheels. A cart had wheels; a sledge did not. The same commentator, cited previously with reference to the threshing floor, also describes sledges and carts:

> Sledges were built of heavy wood, studded underneath with sharp stones, potsherds, or iron spikes. The cart was built with studded rollers. Benches with backrests were built on top for drivers. Sledges were drawn by teams of oxen, donkeys, or horses, and encircled the pile of grain heaped in the center of the threshing floor. Women and men drove the

teams while others with forks raked loose sheaves into the sledge path and raked away the threshed straw. (G. B. Funderburk, *Zondervan Pictorial Encyclopedia of the Bible*, s.v. "threshing floor")

After the stalks were threshed, there still remained the task of separating the grain from the straw and chaff. This was accomplished by "winnowing." Ideally the threshing floor was located on top of a hill or mound so as to take advantage of the wind. Throwing the mixture up into the air with a fork or shovel allowed the chaff to be blown away, while the heavier kernels of grain fell back to the threshing floor. There the grain could be gathered, bagged, and stored, whereas the chaff was gathered and burned.

The picture of useless chaff being burned serves as the basis for a stern warning John the Baptist issues to the Pharisees and Sadducees. They came out to the Jordan to hear his preaching, but they refused to accept his message of repentance and faith in the Lamb of God, who was just then appearing on the scene. John warns them of their precarious position. Drawing on a familiar scene from the threshing floor, he tells them:

> *"I baptize you with water for repentance. But after me will come one who is more powerful than I, whose sandals I am not fit to carry. He will baptize you with the Holy Spirit and with fire. His winnowing fork is in his hand, and he will clear his threshing floor, gathering his wheat into the barn and burning up the chaff with unquenchable fire."* (Matthew 3:11,12)

John describes in picture language what the writer to the Hebrews says in straightforward terms when he writes, "It is a dreadful thing to fall into the hands of the living God" (Hebrews 10:31).

Growing Figs

And [Jesus] left [the chief priests and teachers of the law] and went out of [Jerusalem] to Bethany, where he spent the night.

Early in the morning, as he was on his way back to the city, he was hungry. Seeing a fig tree by the road, he went up to it but found nothing on it except leaves. Then he said to it, "May you never bear fruit again!" Immediately the tree withered.

When the disciples saw this, they were amazed. "How did the fig tree wither so quickly?" they asked. (Matthew 21:17-20)

Figs were an important addition to the diet of every Jewish family. The fruit grew on a woody shrub that, when cultivated, could reach a height of 20 to 30 feet. A prominent feature of the tree was its large, deeply lobed leaves measuring up to 10 inches across. Recall that Adam and Eve plucked off fig leaves to cover themselves in God's presence. A happier use of the large leaves was providing welcome shade against the blazing Mediterranean sun. When Jesus called Nathanael to be one of his followers, Jesus impressed the cautious disciple with the observation, "I saw you while you were still under the fig tree before Philip called you" (John 1:48). Indeed, sitting under one's own vine and fig tree was an Old Testament picture of peace and prosperity. "During Solomon's lifetime Judah and Israel, from Dan to Beersheba, lived in safety, each man under his own vine and fig tree" (1 Kings 4:25).

On Monday after Palm Sunday, Jesus was walking with his disciples. It was in the spring of the year—Passover time—when Jerusalem was overflowing with pilgrims who totally overwhelmed the lodging accommodations available in the city. Hence, pilgrims camped out wherever they could find space.

Jesus stayed in the area of Bethany on Palm Sunday evening. On Monday morning, Jesus headed back to Jerusalem without having had his breakfast. Upon seeing a fig tree *in leaf*, it was reasonable to expect that it would have some fruit on it. This is because fig trees produced fruit before they leafed out.

Research of horticultural sites on the Internet provides a bewildering array of fruit-bearing patterns among the some 150 varieties of figs cultivated around the world. In harsher climates the fig tree bears fruit only once, whereas the more common pattern is to bear twice per growing season. The first crop (winter figs) grows on "old" wood from the previous growing season. The main crop (summer figs) grows on "new" wood.

Life in the New Testament World

The *Zondervan Pictorial Encyclopedia of the Bible* gives a helpful summary:

> In the East the fig tree produces two definite crops of fruit per season. The normal winter figs ripen in May and June and the summer figs in late August and September. Sometimes, one crop overlaps the other. The baby fruit buds are usually seen in February before the leaves appear in April each year. (s.v. "fig tree")

Jesus' response to the fig tree's "deception" of being in full leaf but having no fruit was to pronounce a curse on it. Consequently, it dried up "immediately." It was not that the green leaves suddenly turned brown before their very eyes. Rather, Mark's account tells us that it was the next morning (Tuesday of Holy Week) that the disciples noticed the tree had withered. Anyone who has observed Dutch elm disease or the emerald ash borer destroying a tree knows it is a long process. For such destruction to happen in one day may fairly be called immediate.

Of the many miracles Jesus did (creating wine, feeding the five thousand, healing the sick, curing the lame, raising the dead), this was the only miracle that was destructive. A likely explanation is that Jesus was using the incident as an object lesson to teach his disciples what must, out of necessity, happen to faithless and fruitless people.

If anyone has the uncomfortable feeling that Jesus was planning to steal some fruit for his breakfast or that Jesus could be labeled a vandal for blasting someone's fig tree, he or she can rest easy on both counts. Matthew inserts the significant detail that this tree was "by the road."

There was an Old Testament Levitical regulation that gave travelers the right to help themselves to the grain or fruit they could reach from the path. So, if there had been fruit on the tree, it would have been permissible for Jesus to pick it for himself and his disciples. Furthermore, by being "by the road," the tree was likely in the public domain, not in someone's private orchard. Barren and ownerless, the tree deserved the fate Jesus had outlined in an earlier parable of a barren fig tree. There he had the owner of the barren tree saying: "Cut it down! Why should it use up the soil?" (Luke 13:7).

Mustard

Again [Jesus] said, "What shall we say the kingdom of God is like, or what parable shall we use to describe it? It is like a mustard seed, which is the smallest seed you plant in the ground. Yet when planted, it grows and becomes the largest of all garden plants, with such big branches that the birds of the air can perch in its shade." (Mark 4:30-32)

Weeds can be found everywhere. Dandelions, crabgrass, thistles, quack grass—all thrive in our lawns and burden our fields. The mustard plant is also included among our native weed population. A pile of topsoil stored on a construction site or in a neglected corner of a field is likely to spring up a bed of yellow-flowering mustard plants. But our variety of mustard plant is a problem because it spreads so easily, rather than because the plants become so large.

The mustard plant Jesus has in mind in his parable is different from the mustard plants we are familiar with. Note first of all that this mustard plant is not wild. It is sown in the garden; its seeds are used for food. We're not told in Scripture how the mustard seeds were used, but along with the cummin and caraway seeds Isaiah spoke of, mustard seeds may have served as spices for main dishes or condiments for side dishes.

The mustard plants Jesus was familiar with grew quite large. They are still found in parts of the world. An older commentator tells of mustard plants "attaining the height of horse and rider, as travelers have noted" *(Davis Dictionary of the Bible)*. A photo found on the Internet shows a tall man extending an arm straight up and still failing by about 2 feet to reach the top of the mustard plant, which must be 10 or 12 feet tall.

But Jesus' parable isn't really about mustard. It's a picture of the growth of his church. The gospels make five references to mustard seed, all showing that significant results can come from seemingly small beginnings. Beginning with a very small core of disciples faithfully preaching God's Word, the Christian church has grown into a mighty "tree," with branches reaching into all corners of the world.

With the development of modern information technology, there is no place where the gospel message has not been made available. As such, the growth of the gospel mustard seed is a sign of the end times. Jesus predicted, "This gospel of the kingdom will be preached in the whole world as a testimony to all nations, and then the end will come" (Matthew 24:14). The parable of the mustard tree serves as an earnest reminder for all of us to be busy with our individual opportunities for kingdom work, whether that be with our prayers, our contributions, or our personal testimony.

Fishing

ANGLING

Even a cursory reading of Scripture reveals that fish were a staple in the diet of people living at Jesus' time. The boy's lunch that fed more than five thousand people consisted of five barley loaves and two small fish. Later Jesus fed four thousand people with seven loaves and "a few small fish" (Mark 8:7). In describing a father's concern for his son, Jesus asks, "Which of you, if his son . . . asks for a fish, will give him a snake?" (Matthew 7:9,10). To prove to his disciples, who were hiding behind locked doors, on Easter evening that he was really who he claimed to be, Jesus accepted and ate a piece of broiled fish before them. But perhaps most indicative of the prominence of fishing in the life of New Testament people is that at least seven of Jesus' disciples (John 21:2) were fishermen. Their initial call to discipleship and their reinstatement as disciples were both marked by a miraculous catch of fish (Luke 5:1-11; John 21:1-14).

But how were fish caught in New Testament times? It would appear most were netted. However, there are also references to taking individual fish, both by spearing and by angling. Among the pictures preserved from ancient Egypt is one depicting a man on a papyrus raft holding a spear in his hand, obviously stalking fish in the Nile.

Though there are in Scripture no specific instances of spearing fish, there is reference to the basic equipment for doing so. Challenging Job, God asks him in regard to the dreaded, amphibious "leviathan" (crocodile), "Can you fill his hide with harpoons or his head with fishing spears?" (Job 41:7). The same is true for angling work. God challenges Job, "Can you pull in the leviathan with a fishhook?" (Job 41:1).

The crocodile is an inappropriate quarry for angling, but fish can be caught that way. Matthew records an example of that method being used by Peter on the shore of the Sea of Galilee:

> *After Jesus and his disciples arrived in Capernaum, the collectors of the two-drachma tax came to Peter and asked, "Doesn't your teacher pay the temple tax?"*
>
> *"Yes, he does," he replied.*
>
> *When Peter came into the house, Jesus was the first to speak. "What do you think, Simon?" he asked. "From whom do the kings of the earth collect duty and taxes—from their own sons or from others?"*
>
> *"From others," Peter answered.*
>
> *"Then the sons are exempt," Jesus said to him. "But so that we may not offend them, go to the lake and throw out your line. Take the first fish you catch; open its mouth and you will find a four-drachma coin. Take it and give it to them for my tax and yours."*
>
> (Matthew 17:24-27)

There will be occasion later to discuss the coins in circulation in New Testament times, but we do need to take a look at the tax that was expected of Jesus and his disciples when they returned to Capernaum, where their citizenship was likely registered.

The origin of what came to be called the temple tax dated back to the time of the exodus. Moses writes in the book of Exodus:

> *Then the LORD said to Moses, "When you take a census of the Israelites to count them, each one must pay the LORD a ransom for his life at the time he is counted. Then no plague will come on them when you number them. Each one who crosses over to those already counted is to give a half shekel, according to the sanctuary shekel, which weighs twenty gerahs. This half shekel is an offering to the LORD. All who cross over, those twenty years old or more, are to give an offering to the LORD. The rich are not to give more than a half shekel and the poor are not to give less when you make the offering to the LORD to atone for your lives. Receive the atonement money from the Israelites and use it for the service of the Tent of Meeting. It will be a memorial*

for the Israelites before the LORD, *making atonement for your lives."* (Exodus 30:11-16)

Every man 20 years and older was required to "pay the LORD a ransom for his life." Initially used to give financial support to the tabernacle, at Christ's time it had come to be used for the temple and its services.

Paying "atonement" money to effect a "ransom for his life" was not really applicable to Jesus, who already was the Son of God. Nor was it necessary for his disciples, who by virtue of their connection to Christ by faith were *adopted* sons of God. Technically, as sons of the kingdom they would not have been liable for the tax, but as Christ pointed out, not paying it would almost certainly have been misunderstood. To avoid even the appearance of disrespect for the temple, Jesus instructed Peter how to get the money needed to satisfy the tax collector.

The NIV translates, "Go to the lake and throw out your line." Literally, the text says, "Throw out a hook." The Greek word used is *angkistron,* related to the word *angkale,* which has the base meaning of "something bent at an angle," hence, "a hook." In the Greek word we see the basis for speaking of hook-and-line fishing as "angling."

Critics have scoffed at this account as merely a variation on a number of ancient tales that speak of treasure being found in the mouth of a fish. There is, of course, no reason to doubt that the Creator-God could use this method to address a current problem and supply a miraculous solution. As for the fish, the bearer of the valuable "cargo," the gospel account gives no indication of whether Peter rewarded it by practicing catch-and-release or whether he took it home for dinner.

THE DRAGNET

It's clear from the New Testament that taking fish by hook and line or by spearing was known and practiced. But taking one fish at a time was a rather labor-intensive method of gaining food for the table. Greater efficiency could be achieved by catching fish in numbers. Hence, the more common practice of netting fish. In the gospel there are three different words for *net,* thereby indicating some variety in net construction and use and indicating how important this method of fishing was.

Perhaps the type of net we are most inclined to think of is the dragnet (Greek: *sagene*). Let out from a boat, it was a large, open-mouthed pouch that was dragged over the bottom of the lake so as to enclose bottom-dwelling fish. The forward motion of the boat kept the targeted fish in the net until it could be pulled up on shore. There the fishermen sorted out the "keepers" and disposed of the "culls." Such a dragnet, or seine, catching all sorts of fish, forms the framework of one of Jesus' parables describing the kingdom of heaven. Matthew writes:

> *"Once again, the kingdom of heaven is like a net that was let down into the lake and caught all kinds of fish. When it was full, the fishermen pulled it up on the shore. Then they sat down and collected the good fish in baskets, but threw the bad away. This is how it will be at the end of the age. The angels will come and separate the wicked from the righteous and throw them into the fiery furnace, where there will be weeping and gnashing of teeth."* (Matthew 13:47-50)

A variation of the dragnet was used to catch suspended, or surface-feeding, fish. This net was dragged along the surface of the water instead of along the bottom. It consisted of a long, flat panel of netting (think of a tennis court net perhaps 100 yards long) that was held at the water's surface by a series of wooden floats attached to the top edge of the net and weighed down by lead weights attached to the bottom border of the net. With one end of the net held by someone standing in the water close to shore, or with a net let out from a boat, a second boat would then make a wide semicircular sweep to encircle the unsuspecting fish that would be enclosed when the two ends of the net were drawn up on the shore.

Casting Nets

A decidedly different approach to netting fish was the use of a smaller, one-man casting net *(amphiblestron)*. It was this kind of net that Peter and Andrew were using when Jesus first invited them to follow him. Matthew says:

> As Jesus was walking beside the Sea of Galilee, he saw two brothers, Simon called Peter and his brother Andrew. They were casting a net into the lake, for they were fishermen. "Come, follow me," Jesus said, "and I will make you fishers of men." At once they left their nets and followed him. (Matthew 4:18-20)

No example of an item so fragile as a casting net remains from ancient times, but the method is still very much in use today with equipment that is not likely to have changed much over the centuries. Participants in the Wisconsin Lutheran Seminary archaeological dig, mentioned previously, regularly observed local fishermen wading out waist deep at dusk and casting their nets in search of the small, sardinelike fish common in the Mediterranean.

An Internet article describes a contemporary version of the casting net as follows:

> A cast net, also called a throw net, is a net used for fishing. It is a circular net with small weights distributed around its edge. The net is cast or thrown by hand in such a manner that it spreads out on the water and sinks. . . . Fish are caught as the net is hauled back in. This simple device has been in use, with various modifications, for thousands of years. (wikipedia.org, search "cast net")

In speaking of the construction and technique involved in using the net, the same article continues:

> Contemporary cast nets have a radius which ranges from 4 to 12 feet. Only strong people can lift the larger nets once they are filled with fish. Standard nets for recreational fishing have a 4-foot hoop. Weights are usually distributed around the edge at about one pound per foot. Attached to the net is a landline, one end of which is held in the hand as the net is thrown. When the net is full, a retrieval clamp, which works like a wringer on a mop, closes the net around the fish. The net is then retrieved by pulling on the landline. The net is lifted into a bucket and the clamp is released, dumping the caught fish into the bucket.

Cast nets work best in water no deeper than their radius. Casting is best done in waters free of obstructions. Reeds cause tangles and branches can rip nets. The net caster stands with one hand holding the landline, and with the net draped over the other arm, so the weights dangle. The line is then thrown out to the water, using both hands, in a circular motion rather as in hammer throwing. The net can be cast from a boat, or from the shore, or by wading. (wikipedia.org, search "cast net")

A third term used in the New Testament for *net* is the word *diktyon*. It serves as a generic term for any kind of net—even those used for catching birds or animals.

This word is used in two accounts recorded in the gospels describing miraculous catches of fish on the Sea of Galilee. One takes place at the beginning of the Twelve's discipleship. The other takes place at the end, when Jesus appears to them at the Sea of Galilee after his resurrection. If we read those accounts with our understanding of the types of nets used by the fishermen of the day, we come up with some interesting possibilities.

The first account is recorded in Luke 5:1-11. Luke writes:

One day as Jesus was standing by the Lake of Gennesaret, with the people crowding around him and listening to the word of God, he saw at the water's edge two boats, left there by the fishermen, who were washing their nets. He got into one of the boats, the one belonging to Simon, and asked him to put out a little from shore. Then he sat down and taught the people from the boat.

When he had finished speaking, he said to Simon, "Put out into deep water, and let down the nets for a catch."

Simon answered, "Master, we've worked hard all night and haven't caught anything. But because you say so, I will let down the nets."

When they had done so, they caught such a large number of fish that their nets began to break. So they signaled their partners in the other boat to come and help them, and they came and filled both boats so full that they began to sink.

When Simon Peter saw this, he fell at Jesus' knees and said, "Go away from me, Lord; I am a sinful man!" For he and all his companions

> were astonished at the catch of fish they had taken, and so were James and John, the sons of Zebedee, Simon's partners.
>
> Then Jesus said to Simon, "Don't be afraid; from now on you will catch men." So they pulled their boats up on shore, left everything and followed him.

Jesus said, "Put out into deep water, and let down the nets [*diktya*, plural] for a catch." The command was given to Peter, but from the context, it's apparent there were other crew members with him. Note especially Christ's use of the plural *nets*. It seems highly unlikely for Peter's boat to put out two or more nets of the large, dragnet variety. Note also that the nets Peter put out could be emptied while the boats were still out on the water, so as to fill two boats. By contrast, recall that a dragnet had to be drawn up on shore to collect the catch. If indeed the *diktya* Peter was operating with were casting nets (intended for taking small fish in shallow water during times of low light), then the miraculous aspects of this catch become even more dramatic. Using the wrong equipment at the wrong time of day in the wrong place yielded a catch big enough to swamp two boats! It's no wonder "[Peter] and all his companions were astonished at the catch of fish they had taken."

The gospel writer John records the second of the two miracles:

> Afterward Jesus appeared again to his disciples, by the Sea of Tiberias. It happened this way: Simon Peter, Thomas (called Didymus), Nathanael from Cana in Galilee, the sons of Zebedee, and two other disciples were together. "I'm going out to fish," Simon Peter told them, and they said, "We'll go with you." So they went out and got into the boat, but that night they caught nothing.
>
> Early in the morning, Jesus stood on the shore, but the disciples did not realize that it was Jesus.
>
> He called out to them, "Friends, haven't you any fish?"
>
> "No," they answered.
>
> He said, "Throw your net on the right side of the boat and you will find some." When they did, they were unable to haul the net in because of the large number of fish.

> *Then the disciple whom Jesus loved said to Peter, "It is the Lord!" As soon as Simon Peter heard him say, "It is the Lord," he wrapped his outer garment around him (for he had taken it off) and jumped into the water. The other disciples followed in the boat, towing the net full of fish, for they were not far from shore, about a hundred yards. When they landed, they saw a fire of burning coals there with fish on it, and some bread.*
>
> *Jesus said to them, "Bring some of the fish you have just caught."*
>
> *Simon Peter climbed aboard and dragged the net ashore. It was full of large fish, 153, but even with so many the net was not torn.* (John 21:1-11)

The miraculous catch of fish at the close of Jesus' stay on earth also uses the generic term *diktyon* for *net*, but the circumstances surrounding this catch are different. For one thing, the singular *net*, not *nets*, is used. This could well be a large dragnet. Note that the full net was drawn up on shore and emptied of its catch, typical of the method employed with a dragnet.

Granted, the two accounts are similar, but the differences in details do serve a purpose. Critics are prone to say that there was only one catch of fish and that Luke and John are describing the same thing in somewhat garbled form. The subtle difference in the fishing equipment used is just one of a number of details establishing that these are in fact two different miracles.

Fish

> *When Jesus looked up and saw a great crowd coming toward him, he said to Philip, "Where shall we buy bread for these people to eat?" He asked this only to test him, for he already had in mind what he was going to do.*
>
> *Philip answered him, "Eight months' wages would not buy enough bread for each one to have a bite!"*
>
> *Another of his disciples, Andrew, Simon Peter's brother, spoke up, "Here is a boy with five small barley loaves and two small fish, but how far will they go among so many?"* (John 6:5-9)

> *When they landed, they saw a fire of burning coals there with fish on it, and some bread.*
>
> *Jesus said to them, "Bring some of the fish you have just caught."*
>
> *Simon Peter climbed aboard and dragged the net ashore. It was full of large fish, 153, but even with so many the net was not torn. Jesus said to them, "Come have breakfast."* (John 21:9-12)

With all the talk about nets, it's fair to ask, "What kind of fish were netted?" While the Scriptures do not identify specific species by name, they do give us a range of sizes. The fish vary from the "two small fish" multiplied by Jesus to feed more than five thousand people to the 153 "large fish" taken by Peter's party upon the helpful advice of the risen Lord.

Technically, in the account of the feeding of the five thousand, the term used to describe what was in the boy's lunch is a word that means "something cooked." Hence, it's the fixings for a sandwich, what was eaten with the bread. Often the sandwich ingredient was some form of fish, and so the word meaning "something cooked" came to be used for "fish." In his account John uses the diminutive of the word, so the translation "two *small* fish" is an appropriate translation.

At the other end of the spectrum were the 153 "*large* fish" Jesus graciously provided to Peter and his crew.

An ancient commentator, enumerating the species and subspecies of fish found in the Sea of Galilee, listed 22 varieties. Modern estimates range from 25 to 35 species. Not all of these, however, were found in ancient times. Pond raising of carp, for example, is of fairly recent origin. Most authorities, however, agree that from ancient times there have been three basic categories of fish.

The smallest fish generally taken for food are members of the Mediterranean sardine family. These small, smeltlike fish are the quarry that sport fishermen are usually pursuing when they venture out into the surf with their casting nets.

The largest fish, sometimes growing to a length of 3 feet or more, are barbel. As indicated by their name, they have barbs on both sides of their heads, thus putting them into the catfish/bullhead family. Lacking fins and scales, they would have been unclean and not fit for Jewish consumption, pursuant to the Old Testament regulation spelled out in Leviticus 11:9,10: "'Of all the creatures living in the water of the seas and the streams, you may eat any that have fins and scales. But all creatures in the seas or streams that do not have fins and scales . . . you are to detest.'"

The third major category is the tilapia family and its many subcategories. Some of these varieties grow quite large. One current source says, "This tasty fish could measure up to a foot and a half long and weigh 3.3 pounds." Most of the varieties, however, are smaller panfish, very similar in size and appearance to the black crappie common in American waters. No trip to Israel is complete without tasting the tilapia featured on restaurant menus as "St. Peter's fish." The tour guide's explanation of the name, of course, is that this is the fish that supplied Peter with the coin he needed for paying the temple tax. Perhaps!

As noted above, tilapia do get bigger than the plate-sized ones served to tourists, so the 153 large fish that Jesus provided in the miraculous catch John reports may have been this prized food fish.

Incidentally, in connection with John's account of the breakfast scene, there is a misunderstanding that could easily result from some of the translations of verse 10. In the NIV quoted previously, Jesus' directive to the disciples is translated, "Bring some of the fish you have just caught." Recall that when the fishermen came in off the lake, Jesus already had fish and bread for their breakfast going over a fire. The translation "bring some of the fish you have just caught" could sound as though Jesus wanted to add more fish to what was on the grill. A careful look at the original, however, suggests that Jesus is urging them to sort out the catch. He's saying, "Take some of the fish (as keepers) and return the rest to the lake. Then come and have your breakfast."

Perhaps Jesus was trying to avoid waste. Currently there is considerable encouragement from environmentalists to "go green" by avoiding waste. It is informative to note that the Creator-God, who owns everything and needs nothing, has always been concerned about avoiding waste. As evidence for that statement, look at Jesus' procedure after feeding the five thousand, where he had the disciples pick up 12 baskets of leftovers, or after feeding the four thousand, where they picked up 7 baskets. It would only be consistent for Jesus to urge a "green" course of action: first to take care of the valuable catch, and then to enjoy breakfast.

Just as the nutritious fish from the Sea of Galilee could sustain physical bodies, so also the symbolism attached to the word *fish* can sustain the soul. The five-letter Greek word that spells *fish* (*i-ch-th-u-s*) came to symbolize the Christian faith. The five letters in the word *fish* are the first letters of the five-word Christian confession: *Jesus Christ God's Son, Savior.*

In the early church, the stylized picture of a fish became a code to identify if a person was a Christian. We still see the fish symbol commonly used in our day, either as decoration for our homes or as a public statement displayed on the back of a vehicle. What a significant change from New Testament times when the sign of the fish must have seemed to unchristian neighbors as mere street graffiti!

Publishing

Of making many books there is no end, and much study wearies the body. (Ecclesiastes 12:12)

Reflecting a measure of weariness, Solomon observes that the sheer volume of books produced in his day was enough to tire out the diligent reader.

What would he say of our day when anybody with a computer and a printer can launch into desktop publishing? With the click of a button, we can bring up any number of copies, in color or black and white, outfitted with page numbers and footnotes, enhanced with pictures and charts, etc. Even Gutenberg's relatively cumbersome press (developed in the 1450s), featuring moveable type, was a great improvement over the publishing technology of Solomon's time.

In Solomon's time and extending far into the New Testament era, every page had to be copied by hand—manually. Hence, the term *manu-script* for a product that resulted from hand copying.

That Solomon could feel burdened by the volume of material produced by this relatively inefficient method is not only surprising but also a tribute to the patience and industry of an important class of workers, namely the professional writers, or scribes.

SCRIBES

Little is known about early hand copying of the Torah (the five books of Moses). An increase in the activity of hand copying seems to correspond to the time of Israel's return to Jerusalem after their 70-year captivity in Babylon. A key figure in this movement was the scribe Ezra. Scripture says of him, "Ezra went up from Babylon, and he was a scribe skilled in the law of Moses, which the LORD God of Israel had given" (Ezra 7:6, NASB). His reading of the law in the presence of all the people greatly increased interest in producing copies of the five books of Moses, as well as the other Old Testament books, all of which required hand copying.

One cannot help but be impressed by how seriously the returning exiles took the law as it was read to them by Ezra (Nehemiah 8:1–10:39). That type of reverence for the Word showed itself in the almost obsessive respect scribes came to display in their methods of copying the Scriptures. Eventually there developed a set of rigid guidelines scribes were expected to follow in their work. An Internet post lists nine requirements for scribes to follow:

1. They could only use clean animal skins, both to write on, and even to bind manuscripts.
2. Each column of writing could have no less than forty-eight, and no more than sixty lines.
3. The ink must be black, and of a special recipe.
4. They must verbalize each word aloud while they were writing.
5. They must wipe the pen and wash their entire bodies before writing the word "Jehovah," every time they wrote it.
6. There must be a review within thirty days, and if as many as three pages required corrections, the entire manuscript had to be redone.
7. The letters, words, and paragraphs had to be counted, and the document became invalid if two letters touched

each other. The middle paragraph, word and letter must correspond to those of the original document.

8. The documents could be stored only in sacred places (synagogues, etc).

9. As no document containing God's Word could be destroyed, they were stored, or buried, in a genizah [a Hebrew term meaning "hiding place, " usually in a synagogue or sometimes in a Jewish cemetery]. (wikipedia.org, search "scribe")

Hand copying is always susceptible to errors, but it is immediately apparent that under such strict guidelines the Old Testament scribes produced very accurate copies. These copies of the Old Testament were, of course, very important because in the beginning they were the only Bible the New Testament Christian church had until the gospels and epistles were given by the Holy Spirit.

The New Testament church soon used scribes also. At the end of Galatians (6:11), Paul seems to be affixing his signature to this book that had been written down by a secretary or scribe. Romans 16:22 informs us that the secretary who recorded Paul's message for the Romans was Tertius, and he includes his greetings to the readers.

Scribes soon began to make copies of all of Paul's letters for use in the various congregations. Like Tertius, these scribes likely were Christian and very conscientious about their copying. However, lacking the rigid guidelines that bound the Old Testament scribes, it is not surprising that the Greek New Testament manuscripts have more variants (small differences in the text) than does the Old Testament Hebrew text.

The writing materials of the Old Testament scribes and the New Testament copyists would have been very similar. Mundane, secular subject matter was regularly written on a form of paper made from papyrus, a rushlike plant native to Egypt. More important subject matter, and especially religious writing, was written on a scraped leather surface. Sheepskin or goatskin was the ordinary source for this parchment writing surface.

Both papyrus and parchment had a good side and a less good side. Thin strips of papyrus fiber were laid out on a flat surface in crosshatch fashion and then dried to make a tolerable writing surface. The side where the papyrus fiber lay horizontally was the better side. The leather-based parchment was very smooth on the flesh side of the skin; less so on the side from which the hair had been scraped. Hence, both papyrus and parchment manuscripts were usually written on only one side.

The writing surface determined which kind of "pen" was used. A sharp quill pen worked fine for the hard, smooth parchment surface, whereas it would have dug into the softer and rougher papyrus surface. On papyrus the writing was done with a *stylus*, a small brush something like our fiber-tipped pens. In either case, the writing tool would be dipped into ink made with lampblack, usually obtained from burned wood, but sometimes from burned nutshells.

Until the invention of the *codex* book form (individual sheets spine-bound like our books), individual pieces of papyrus or parchment were usually bound together to make one long strip. This could then be rolled up as a *scroll* for storage and unrolled for reading. Luke gives us a glimpse of how that worked:

> *[Jesus] went to Nazareth, where he had been brought up, and on the Sabbath day he went into the synagogue, as was his custom. And he stood up to read. The scroll of the prophet Isaiah was handed to him. Unrolling it, he found the place where it is written:*
>
> *"The Spirit of the Lord is on me, because he has anointed me to preach good news to the poor. He has sent me to proclaim freedom for the prisoners and recovery of sight for the blind, to release the oppressed, to proclaim the year of the Lord's favor."*
>
> *Then he rolled up the scroll, gave it back to the attendant and sat down.* (Luke 4:16-20)

Lying in prison in Rome and awaiting a martyr's death, Paul requests of his coworker Timothy, "When you come bring the cloak which I left at Troas with Carpus, and the books, especially the parchments" (2 Timothy 4:13, NASB).

Paul seems to be making a distinction between the books and the parchments, but it is impossible to determine what the difference was and whether the books were in scroll or codex form. There are those who maintain that binding copied material into codex form was a uniquely Christian innovation.

The specific term *papyrus* is not used in the New Testament, but there seems to be a clear alternate term for it. At the end of his second epistle, John says, "Although having many things to write to you, I do not want to do it with chartou and ink." (Note that our word *chart* is related to the term *chartou.*) The NIV translates, "I have much to write to you, but I do not want to use paper and ink" (2 John 12). Paper is actually a later Chinese invention. John is likely referring to papyrus.

Judging from the restrictions under which the Old Testament scribe worked, he is likely to have worked alone, copying from a master copy *(exemplar)* at his side. New Testament scribes could work in the same way, but there soon came into being a method of reproducing multiple copies at the same time. That advancement was the arrival of the *scriptorium.* In appearance, it would have seemed like a classroom, with people sitting at desks and a person standing at a lectern. But instead of teaching, the person at the lectern would be reading, slowly and distinctly, so that the listeners at their desks could copy down what they heard.

Both methods allowed mistakes to creep in. The person working alone at his manuscript and looking across to his exemplar could see something incorrectly and copy a mistake into his manuscript. If there was any kind of noise or disturbance, the copyist at his desk in the scriptorium could hear something incorrectly and enter a wrong word. On balance, however, it is not surprising that an occasional error crept in. Rather, what surprises is the remarkable accuracy of handwritten manuscripts.

Lawyers and Teachers of the Law

Then Jesus said to the crowds and to his disciples: "The teachers of the law and the Pharisees sit in Moses' seat. So you must obey them and do everything they tell you. But do not do what they do, for they do not practice what they preach. They tie up heavy loads and put them on men's shoulders, but they themselves are not willing to lift a finger to move them.

> *"Everything they do is done for men to see: They make their phylacteries wide and the tassels on their garments long; they love the place of honor at banquets and the most important seats in the synagogues; they love to be greeted in the marketplaces and to have men call them 'Rabbi.'"* (Matthew 23:1-7)

The words cited above are the introduction to the seven woes Jesus directed toward the religious leadership of his day. These were the "teachers of the law," primarily the lawyers and the Pharisees.

Actually, the term *lawyer* is not used here. It occurs only a few times in the New Testament—once in Matthew and six times in Luke. Likewise, the term *teachers of the law* is not used here. That term, when referring to Jewish teachers, occurs only in Luke 5:17 and Acts 5:34. In the overwhelming number of instances where translators have used the term *teachers of the law*, they are opting for that as their translation of the word *scribes*. The Hebrew word for *scribe* occurs some 50 times in the Old Testament. In the New Testament, it is used over 60 times.

The extension of the term *scribe* to allow the meaning of "lawyer" or "teacher of the law" is a very understandable development. A scribe's careful copying of the Torah, the five books of the Law, soon made him thoroughly familiar with their content. This enabled him to quote and interpret for others the many laws that came to mark Jewish life. A modern commentator says that about the scribe's dual role of copyist and interpreter:

> Since every detail of Jewish life was expected to be regulated by the law, and since it was impossible for an ordinary Jew to become familiar with the multitude of legal requirements and to apply them in the new situations of daily life, it was absolutely necessary for some men to devote themselves to a study of the law. Those who did were the lawyers.
>
> Among the leading duties of the lawyers were the following: to study, interpret, and expound the law; to teach the law in the schools and in the synagogues; to decide questions of law; to act as judges. (J. L. Kelso, *Zondervan Pictorial Encyclopedia of the Bible*, s.v. "lawyer")

Note the mixed review that Jesus gives these "teachers of the law." On the positive side he says, "The teachers of the law and the Pharisees sit in Moses' seat. So you must obey them and do everything they tell you" (Matthew 23:2,3). Jesus credits them with accurately reproducing the content of God's Old Testament revelation. And we need to remember that the Old Testament was the only Bible that existed in Jesus' day.

What they did with retaining the Old Testament message was fine, but their application of it was dreadfully faulty. Jesus warns his listeners: "So you must obey them and do everything they tell you. But do not do what they do, for they do not practice what they preach."

In addition to God's *revealed* Law, given on Mount Sinai, the scribers and Pharisees maintained there was also inspired *oral* law, or tradition. This oral tradition added many rules and regulations to Jewish daily life. The leaders themselves did not keep these rules, but they required rank-and-file Jews to do so.

Jesus becomes more specific in his indictment:

They tie up heavy loads and put them on men's shoulders, but they themselves are not willing to lift a finger to move them. Everything they do is done for men to see: They make their phylacteries wide and the tassels on their garments long; they love the place of honor at banquets and the most important seats in the synagogues; they love to be greeted in the marketplaces and to have men call them "Rabbi." (Matthew 23:4-7)

It is impossible not to sense the indignation Jesus feels toward these religious leaders as he directs against them the broadside of seven woes, branding them as "hypocrites," "snakes," and a "brood of vipers."

Although Jesus blasts the scribes of his day, it is interesting and instructive—with the benefit of historical hindsight—to see how God subsequently used this cadre of skillful scribes for his own good purpose. After the destruction of Jerusalem by the Romans in A.D. 70, the whole system that Jesus denounced during his ministry was totally displaced. Instead of operating in Jerusalem, the scribes retired to the city of Tiberius in lightly regarded "Galilee of the Gentiles" (see Matthew 4:15). Here, in addition to devoting themselves to the study and elaboration of oral tradition, they continued their zeal for carefully copying the Old Testament Scriptures. The result of their work was that accurate copies of the Hebrew Old Testament continued to be available until the advent of printing in the Middle Ages, which eliminated the need for hand copying.

When the Dead Sea Scrolls were discovered in 1947, they gave the world a biblical text that was copied almost a thousand years earlier than any of the Old Testament manuscripts previously available. Together with other content, these newly found scrolls contain all or portions of all the canonical Old Testament Scriptures except the book of Esther. There is remarkable agreement between these much earlier Dead Sea Scrolls (some written as early as 100 B.C.) and the later hand-copied manuscripts that served until they were replaced by printed versions in medieval times.

Obviously, we have here a clear-cut example of God preserving his Word. That should not surprise us. After all, he has promised, "Heaven and earth will pass away, but my words will never pass away" (Matthew 24:35).

Teaching

Only be careful, and watch yourselves closely so that you do not forget the things your eyes have seen or let them slip from your heart as long as you live. Teach them to your children and to their children after them. (Deuteronomy 4:9)

When Moses stepped down from leading Israel, he gave Jewish fathers a very weighty assignment. He made them responsible for teaching their children the great things God had done for them in leading them out of Egypt. This they were expected to accomplish by what today we would call homeschooling. There is no indication that formal classroom instruction existed prior to the arrival of the institution of the synagogue much later in Jewish history.

When did the synagogue start? Although specific dates are uncertain, there is general consensus that it began during the Babylonian captivity, which began in 586 B.C. Deprived of access to the temple in Jerusalem, the captive Jews could no longer observe a worship pattern that offered the formerly prescribed sacrifices. The adjustment the displaced Jews made was to give the Old Testament Scriptures, and especially the Torah, the central place in their religious system. Thus the Jewish nation became a "people of the Book." When the Persian ruler Cyrus permitted the Jews to return to their homeland, many declined the offer and stayed in Babylonia. Some, however, did return to Palestine under the leadership of Ezra and Nehemiah. No doubt they brought their synagogue traditions with them.

In the context of synagogue worship, the reverence given the Torah and the rest of the Old Testament Scriptures bordered on the extreme. Lacking regular clergy, the Jewish community devised a worship system that was essentially a democratic institution. All that was needed for gathering as a group around the Word was a "quorum" made up of ten men. Youths older than 13 years and a day could be included in that quorum. These men took their turns leading the services by reading and explaining selected portions of Scripture.

If notable guests were present, they might be invited to take part. One thinks of Jesus preaching in the synagogue at Nazareth (Luke 4:16) or Paul and Barnabas in Antioch. *Acts* describes the scene:

> *From Perga [Paul and Barnabas] went on to Pisidian Antioch. On the Sabbath they entered the synagogue and sat down. After the reading from the Law and the Prophets, the synagogue rulers sent word to them, saying, "Brothers, if you have a message of encouragement for the people, please speak."* (Acts 13:14,15)

Jews could meet at a synagogue building—and architectural patterns for synagogues soon developed—but there was no absolute requirement regarding where they could meet. The meeting could be held in a public building or in a private home or even outside (for example, in Philippi, Acts 16:13).

It is impossible to overestimate the importance of the synagogue in the life of the Jewish community. It was their worship place, school, library, social center, community hall, soup kitchen in hard times, and even an occasional motel for a stranded traveler.

Synagogue is the Greek word for this distinctly Jewish institution. The Jewish community itself used three names, all reflective of the synagogue's overlapping functions. Jews could call the synagogue a House of Assembly, but it could also be known as a House of Prayer or a House of Study.

Regarding the term *House of Assembly*, a Jewish Web site stresses that the concept of assembly is central to all that happens in the Jewish community:

> The synagogue is a meeting place for Jews, where they share the important facets of their lives with one another and achieve a sense of community. Judaism is a communal religion; the most important events take place in the presence of other people. Priority is given to the community and its needs, and it is incumbent upon the individual to make the needs of the community his/her priority. What is more, individuals are supported by the community, and this happens most effectively when people come together with one another. The synagogue is the place where people meet to pray, study, celebrate, mourn, and socialize. (www.scheinerman.net/judaism/Synagogue/synagogue.html, accessed September 2010)

The term *House of Prayer* conforms most readily to the Christian term *church*. The synagogue conducts worship services in which, with carefully orchestrated reverence and solemnity, prayers are raised and Old Testament Scriptures are read and explained. From ancient times there have been five distinct parts of the service: a call to worship (the *Shema*, see Deuteronomy 6:4), prayers (18 "benedictions"), the reading of the Law, the reading of the Prophets, and the closing benediction.

But interest in the Law, both written and oral, was not restricted to the Sabbath worship service. It continued throughout the week, making the synagogue a House of Study. Indeed, it can be argued that viewing the synagogue as a study hall or school touches on its most significant feature. One needs only to think of the Yiddish-speaking community that for centuries has referred to the synagogue as its *shul*, reflecting, of course, its indebtedness to the German word *Schule*.

Precise dates are hard to establish, but by about 75 B.C. the mixture of homeschooling and synagogue instruction for children evolved into a system of compulsory elementary training for boys. Girls were not necessarily denied an education, but it was administered at home, likely by their mothers.

The curriculum in the elementary system consisted solely of religious study—no science or math, rhetoric or philosophy, or any craft or technical skills courses. The latter were to be learned from the students' fathers. Much of the religious curriculum was imparted by rote teaching, but there was also an emphasis on reading. After all, how could a member of the community take his turn at reading the Scriptures in the synagogue service if he was illiterate?

This compulsory education program left its mark on synagogue architecture. Although there is a recent (September 2009) news release about an archaeological find that is thought to be a first-century synagogue, most synagogues that have been unearthed until now are dated somewhat later than that. They come from a time when synagogue buildings became larger and more elaborate. Almost all of them have a footprint that reveals two major rooms: the larger one, an assembly hall, flanked by a smaller one alongside, likely a classroom.

The education program also brought with it the need for a new class of professionals, namely, teachers. Many of these were drawn from the scribes and Pharisees mentioned in the gospels. But the educational program did not stop with the student's completion of the elementary program, usually at age 15. Promising students were encouraged to seek further instruction at the academy level. These were schools usually headed by famous rabbis who attracted students to themselves. Paul, for example, was a student of the well-known Pharisee Gamaliel. Whereas the elementary school was connected to the synagogue, the academy usually operated in or around the temple. That may give us an added insight into the incident of the 12-year-old Jesus in the temple.

> *Thinking [Jesus] was in their company, [Joseph and Mary] traveled on for a day. Then they began looking for him among their relatives and friends. When they did not find him, they went back to Jerusalem to look for him. After three days they found him in the temple courts, sitting among the teachers, listening to them and asking them questions. Everyone who heard him was amazed at his understanding and his answers.* (Luke 2:44-47)

The academy was a place for deep theological discussion and making fine distinctions. Hence, Jesus was not just a standout student among some beginners at the elementary level. No, one might say he was sitting in on a seminary classroom discussion and not only outshining the other students but baffling even their renowned teachers—as only the God-man would have been able to do.

Rabbinic schools collectively comprising the academy often attracted national attention. That was the case with the House of Hillel and the House of Shamai.

Hillel (ca. 60 B.C.–A.D. 20) was a Babylonian Jew who came to Jerusalem to study under two famous teachers, Shemiah and Abtalion. When he was denied admittance because of his inability to pay the required tuition, he addressed the situation by sitting on the windowsill in an attempt to eavesdrop on the great teachers—a tactic, incidentally, that eventually won him admittance into the classroom. Hillel went on to become a very famous and popular liberal teacher who clashed strongly with his equally famous but stern rival Shamai.

Shamai (ca. 50 B.C.–A.D. 30), a local Judean, was a strict rigorist, interpreting the law in the most severe and demanding way possible. Anecdotes of his rigorism abound, such as his trying to force fasting on his young son on the Day of Atonement. Or on one occasion a Gentile came to the two teachers and asked to have Judaism explained to him "within the time [he] could stand on one foot." Shamai dismissed the seeker out of hand on the grounds that such compression was an insult to the Torah. Hillel reportedly won the man to Judaism with his short and uncomplicated answer: "Do not do to your fellows what is hateful to you; this is the whole law; the rest is commentary; go and learn."

Hillel was the grandfather of Gamaliel, mentioned in Acts chapter 5. It would appear that Gamaliel inherited the more liberal outlook of his grandfather. Recall that the apostles had been arrested by the Jewish authorities for preaching Christ crucified. Ordered to cease and desist, Peter responded, "We must obey God rather than men!" (Acts 5:29). Luke records the exchange that followed upon Peter's unyielding response:

> *When [the Jewish leaders] heard this, they were furious and wanted to put them to death. But a Pharisee named Gamaliel, a teacher of the*

> *law, who was honored by all the people, stood up in the Sanhedrin and ordered that the men be put outside for a little while. Then he addressed them: "Men of Israel, consider carefully what you intend to do to these men. Some time ago Theudas appeared, claiming to be somebody, and about four hundred men rallied to him. He was killed, all his followers were dispersed, and it all came to nothing. After him, Judas the Galilean appeared in the days of the census and led a band of people in revolt. He too was killed, and all his followers were scattered. Therefore, in the present case I advise you: Leave these men alone! Let them go! For if their purpose or activity is of human origin, it will fail. But if it is from God, you will not be able to stop these men; you will only find yourselves fighting against God."*
>
> *His speech persuaded them.* (Acts 5:33-40)

It is hard to imagine that Gamaliel's *laissez-faire* attitude sprang from proper motivation or a kindly attitude toward Christians, but the Lord certainly used his advice for the benefit of the young Christian church.

The great honor and respect shown to notable teachers such as Hillel, Shamai, or Gamaliel had an equally strong opposite effect. It engendered distrust of those who had not been certified through the local academy taught by "name" teachers. Matthew informs us that Jesus was the object of such distrust, as shown by the questioning he was subjected to in the temple during Holy Week:

> *Jesus entered the temple courts, and, while he was teaching, the chief priests and the elders of the people came to him. "By what authority are you doing these things?" they asked. "And who gave you this authority?"* (Matthew 21:23)

Jesus warns his followers that they too could expect such opposition when he says,

> *"A student is not above his teacher, nor a servant above his master. It is enough for the student to be like his teacher, and the servant like his master. If the head of the house has been called Beelzebub, how much more the members of his household!"* (Matthew 10:24,25)

Such opposition did indeed happen early on in the post-Easter ministry of the disciples. When Peter and John, on their way to the temple, healed a lame man, it gave them the opportunity to inform the crowd that this miracle had been done in the name of the risen Christ. Jailed as suspects charged with unauthorized teaching, Peter and John were immediately confronted by the authorities with the question, "By what power or what name did you do this?" (Acts 4:7). Peter's confident Christian confession, coming from a person "unschooled" in the local academy system but rather connected with Jesus, was a cause of astonishment to the authorities:

> *When they saw the courage of Peter and John and realized that they were unschooled, ordinary men, they were astonished and they took note that these men had been with Jesus.* (Acts 4:13)

For the Jewish authorities, the problem was not that Peter and John had attached themselves to a teacher and leader. They themselves did that all the time. The problem was that the disciples had attached themselves to the wrong leader. Having the proper academic and theological credentials made all the difference in the world to them.

Construction Trades

It has been noted that the formal educational system offered through the synagogue in New Testament times had a purely religious curriculum. There were no secular course offerings, nor was any manual training given. The latter was supplied by fathers who took to heart the rabbinic warning: "He who does not teach his son a trade teaches him to be a thief." Fathers trained their sons in the family business or apprenticed their sons to one of the local craftsmen.

There was no lack of skilled artisans to learn from. It is important for us to realize that ancient craftsmen were genuinely skilled artisans. Because of technological advances in our day, we easily come to the questionable conclusion that we have progressed far beyond ancient craftsmen. We may be able to produce things in less time or with less effort, or with somewhat closer tolerances, but the ancients were not lacking in talent and skill.

Already upon their exodus from Egypt, Jewish craftsmen were highly skilled. In connection with the building of the tabernacle, we hear of a great number of craftsmen available for the project. We are told:

> Then Moses said to the Israelites, "See, the LORD has chosen Bezalel . . . and he has filled him with the Spirit of God, with skill, ability and knowledge in all kinds of crafts—to make artistic designs for work in gold, silver and bronze, to cut and set stones, to work in wood and to engage in all kinds of artistic craftsmanship. And he has given both him and Oholiab . . . the ability to teach others. He has filled them with skill to do all kinds of work as craftsmen, designers, embroiderers in blue, purple and scarlet yarn and fine linen, and weavers— all of them master craftsmen and designers. (Exodus 35:30-35)

CARPENTERS

At a later time in history, Isaiah gives us an interesting look into the tools and the work pattern of the pagan woodworker who takes a log, turns half of it into an idol, and uses the rest as fuel for cooking his food or heating his house. Mockingly, Isaiah says, "The carpenter measures with a line and makes an outline with a marker; he roughs it out with chisels and marks it with compasses. He shapes it in the form of man, of man in all his glory, that it may dwell in a shrine" (Isaiah 44:13).

> Coming to his hometown, [Jesus] began teaching the people in their synagogue, and they were amazed. "Where did this man get this wisdom and these miraculous powers?" they asked. "Isn't this the carpenter's son? Isn't his mother's name Mary, and aren't his brothers James, Joseph, Simon and Judas? Aren't all his sisters with us? Where then did this man get all these things?" And they took offense at him. (Matthew 13:54-57)

> Jesus left there and went to his hometown, accompanied by his disciples. When the Sabbath came, he began to teach in the synagogue, and many who heard him were amazed.

> "Where did this man get these things?" they asked. "What's this wisdom that has been given him, that he even does miracles! Isn't this the carpenter? Isn't this Mary's son and the brother of James, Joseph, Judas and Simon? Aren't his sisters here with us?" And they took offense at him. (Mark 6:1-3)

Both Matthew's and Mark's reporting of this incident are quoted to illustrate a basic rule of interpretation. That rule is this: A difference between two accounts of the same incident need not necessarily be a mistake. Matthew reports Jesus being called "the carpenter's son." Mark quotes the crowd as calling him "the carpenter." In the growing unrest among Jesus' listeners, both terms to describe Jesus are likely to have been used. If Joseph was a carpenter, Jesus may fairly be called "the carpenter's son." If Joseph shared his trade skills with Jesus, the crowd may correctly call Jesus "the carpenter." To be sure, there's a difference between what the two gospel writers say, but it's not a mistake. Matthew uses one term, Mark the other. Both are true.

Justin Martyr (ca. A.D. 100–165), an early defender of the Christian faith, describes Jesus as "working as a carpenter when among men, making plows and yokes." Whatever his niche may have been in the woodworking business, Jesus' presence in the shop raises some intriguing questions: Did his chisels always stay sharp? Did he never hit his thumb with a hammer? Did he never saw off a board a little too short? Regardless of what the answers to those questions might be, one thing is certain: Jesus looked just like any other carpenter. So much so that his neighbors took offense when he claimed to be someone special. They questioned his divinity, but they never doubted his humanity.

STONECUTTERS

Palestine has always been more blessed with stone than wood as a building material. Even today, one can see partially finished stone houses along the roadways. They are the weekend projects of amateur stonecutters patiently adding block upon block to their future homes.

Stonecutters in New Testament times, particularly during the heyday of Herod the Great's building projects, developed impressive proficiency and skill—enough to amaze the disciples. Mark tells us:

> As he was leaving the temple, one of his disciples said to him, "Look, Teacher! What massive stones! What magnificent buildings!" (Mark 13:1)

The Jewish historian Josephus states that some of the temple's foundation stones were 37 feet long, 12 feet high, and 18 feet wide

(*Antiquities of the Jews*, 15.11.3). Don't underestimate the skill of ancient stonecutters!

Tent Making

After this, Paul left Athens and went to Corinth. There he met a Jew named Aquila, a native of Pontus, who had recently come from Italy with his wife Priscilla, because Claudius had ordered all the Jews to leave Rome. Paul went to see them, and because he was a tentmaker as they were, he stayed and worked with them. Every Sabbath he reasoned in the synagogue, trying to persuade Jews and Greeks.

When Silas and Timothy came from Macedonia, Paul devoted himself exclusively to preaching, testifying to the Jews that Jesus was the Christ. (Acts 18:1-5)

Tent making is mentioned only this once in the New Testament, and it brings together three people practicing that trade. Paul, moving on ahead of his coworkers Silas and Timothy, took lodging in Corinth with Aquila and Priscilla. Together the three pursued the ancient craft of tent making.

Deserts have no fixed borders. In times of drought, they tend to expand. They contract in times of more abundant rainfall. Hence, nomadic people, moving about with their flocks to eke out a meager existence in that changeable environment, could never settle down in permanent homes. The solution to their problem lay in providing some form of portable housing. Tents served admirably.

The tents were customarily made of durable cloth woven of goats' hair. Such tents, usually open in the front but with enclosed living quarters in the rear, continue to be used today. Granted, it presents something of a culture clash to see a TV antenna or satellite dish perched over the living quarters of a tent, but that ancient housing method still serves well in some areas.

G. B. Funderburk states, "Paul's native province of Cilicia was so noted for its good grade of goats' hair cloth, used largely for tents, that it was exported by the designation of *Cilician cloth*. Paul's skill in this craft probably consisted of the sewing together of the proper lengths of cloth and attaching of ropes and loops" (*Zondervan Pictorial Encyclopedia of the Bible*, s.v. "tentmakers").

There could hardly have been a booming business in tents in Corinth with its permanent dwellings, so perhaps these tents were marketed to outlying areas. Some have suggested that Paul was actually a sailmaker, but that is speculation.

Paul worked at his trade on a part-time basis. He could support himself if he needed to, but full-time ministry was always the ideal. When Silas and Timothy came from Macedonia, likely bringing gifts of money, Paul devoted himself exclusively to preaching. It's a priority Paul defends when he tells the Corinthians that "those who preach the gospel should receive their living from the gospel" (1 Corinthians 9:14). See also Galatians 6:6.

2

Commerce and Trade

Barter

Jesus told his disciples: "There was a rich man whose manager was accused of wasting his possessions. So he called him in and asked him, 'What is this I hear about you? Give an account of your management, because you cannot be manager any longer.'

"The manager said to himself, 'What shall I do now? My master is taking away my job. I'm not strong enough to dig, and I'm ashamed to beg—I know what I'll do so that, when I lose my job here, people will welcome me into their houses.'

"So he called in each one of his master's debtors. He asked the first, 'How much do you owe my master?'

"'Eight hundred gallons of olive oil,' he replied.

"The manager told him, 'Take your bill, sit down quickly, and make it four hundred.'

"Then he asked the second, 'And how much do you owe?'

"'A thousand bushels of wheat,' he replied.

"He told him, 'Take your bill and make it eight hundred.'

"The master commended the dishonest manager because he had acted shrewdly." (Luke 16:1-8)

From time immemorial, some business has always been transacted by bartering, that is, exchanging things of approximately equal value. In the parable of the shrewd manager, debtor A has obviously incurred an obligation that is to be repaid with olive oil. We're not told what occasioned the debt, but coming from an agricultural setting, the debtor offered to pay in produce of the land. Specifically, the text says he had obligated himself to deliver "one hundred *baths* of olive oil."

Finding modern equivalents for ancient weights and measures is notoriously difficult. In its Table of Weights and Measures, the *NIV*

Study Bible states that a *bath* is a liquid measure of six gallons, yet in its translation of Luke 16:6, it renders the debtor's bill of one hundred baths as *eight* hundred gallons. Fortunately, such slippage in numbers is of no consequence as to the point of the parable, which simply illustrates the manager's shrewdness in befriending the debtor with a 50 percent reduction.

A similar thing happens in the account of debtor B, who owes "one hundred *cors* of wheat." The *NIV Study Bible* lists a *cor* as a dry measure of six bushels. How close one hundred cors come to the translators' rendering of "a thousand bushels of wheat" is debatable, but again, the numbers are not the point of the parable. The 20 percent reduction illustrates the shrewdness of the manager.

Both of these debtors operated in an agricultural setting and traded in commodities they produced. With nomadic herdsmen, the medium of exchange would have been sheep or goats or even camels. A bit of the latter remains in the tourist industry even today. It's a rather common ploy on the part of a tour guide to get his group invited into the black goat-hair tent of some local sheik. After treating his guests to a cup of steaming hot tea or strong coffee, the sheik lays eyes on some lady in the group and offers to buy her as an addition to his harem at the price of 10 camels. The tour guide (turned broker) is scandalized at such a low offer and proceeds to haggle with the sheik, who eventually raises his bid to 12 camels, or 15, or whatever. Understandably, the deal is never completed, but it gives onlookers an idea of how business would have been done in New Testament times.

In New Testament times, there was also the possibility of paying with small pieces of precious metal, either silver or gold, or an alloy of the two called *electrum*. These pieces were not standardized in any way, so each piece had to be weighed separately to determine its value. Hence, terms such as *shekel, mina,* and *talent* originally were measures of weight, rather than the names of coins.

The innovation of minting precious metal into uniform coins is usually credited to Croesus, who was king of Lydia (modern Turkey) from 560 to 546 B.C. The idea of coinage was picked up by the Persians, who circulated government certified currency throughout the empire. King Darius, for example, issued a much used coin that came to be called a *daric*.

Life in the New Testament World

Alexander the Great (333 B.C.) conquered the Persian Empire and forced on it his Greek culture and coinage. A basic coin in the Greek monetary system was the *drachma*. One hundred drachmas equaled one mina. Sixty minas equaled one talent.

In New Testament times, the Romans ruled the Mediterranean world and brought their system of coinage, central to which was the *denarius*.

Being allowed to mint their own money was not a privilege open to conquered people. Hence, except for a few very small bronze or copper coins, the Jewish nation did not issue any gold or silver coins in New Testament times. The exception to this pattern was that they struck their own precious metal coins when they were in rebellion against Rome in A.D. 66–70 and 132–135. Instead of having their own precious metal coins, the Jewish people needed to rely on the currency of their foreign neighbors, largely Roman denarii, Greek drachmas, and silver shekels from the Phoenician culture around the city of Tyre.

It is not surprising that Palestine, under Roman domination, dealt mostly with Roman coinage. The coin most frequently mentioned in the New Testament Scriptures is the denarius. Reference to it occurs more than a dozen times. Fortunately, the parable of the farmer hiring help at all hours of the working day gives us a way of computing about what a denarius would be worth in modern times:

> "*The kingdom of heaven is like a landowner who went out early in the morning to hire men to work in his vineyard. He agreed to pay them a denarius for the day and sent them into his vineyard.*
>
> "*About the third hour he went out and saw others standing in the marketplace doing nothing. He told them, 'You also go and work in my vineyard, and I will pay you whatever is right.'* . . .
>
> "*He went out again about the sixth hour and the ninth hour and did the same thing. About the eleventh hour he went out and found still others standing around.* . . .
>
> "*When evening came, the owner of the vineyard said to his foreman, 'Call the workers and pay them their wages, beginning with the last ones hired and going on to the first.'*

Commerce and Trade

> *"The workers who were hired about the eleventh hour came and each received a denarius. So when those came who were hired first, they expected to receive more. But each one of them also received a denarius. When they received it, they began to grumble against the landowner. . . .*
>
> *"But he answered one of them, 'Friend, I am not being unfair to you. Didn't you agree to work for a denarius? Take your pay and go.' . . .*
>
> *"So the last will be first, and the first will be last."* (Matthew 20:1-16, selected verses)

This account corroborates the oft-repeated assumption that a denarius equals the pay for one workday. Granted, that still leaves us with the problem of deciding what average pay for one workday would have been, but it gives us a general indication of what the relative purchasing power of a denarius may have been in New Testament times.

Fortunately, precise calculation of monetary values is not necessary for understanding the significance of Scripture's numerous references to coins. These references generally divide themselves into three rather easily recognized groups. There are some monetary references that obviously refer to large sums. There are some that emphasize the smallness of a coin's value. In other cases, the value of the coin involved is incidental to the subject under discussion. Let's look at a couple of examples.

Large Sums

> *When Jesus looked up and saw a great crowd coming toward him, he said to Philip, "Where shall we buy bread for these people to eat?" He asked this only to test him, for he already had in mind what he was going to do.*
>
> *Philip answered him, "Eight months' wages would not buy enough bread for each one to have a bite!"* (John 6:5-7)

The NIV translators give us a workable interpretive rendering with their handling of Philip's answer. They have him saying, "*Eight months' wages* would not buy enough bread." Literally the text says,

"Bread (costing) two hundred denarii would not be enough." Philip apparently considered this a large amount—too large an expenditure for the disciples to take on.

Something quite similar happens in the NIV's handling of the incident involving a woman who poured perfume on Jesus' head:

> While [Jesus] was in Bethany, reclining at the table in the home of a man known as Simon the Leper, a woman came with an alabaster jar of very expensive perfume, made of pure nard. She broke the jar and poured the perfume on his head.
>
> Some of those present were saying indignantly to one another, "Why this waste of perfume? It could have been sold for more than a year's wages and the money given to the poor." (Mark 14:3-5)

Literally the complainers say, "Why wasn't this perfume sold for three hundred denarii?" If we figure a standard work year to be about 250 days, then the translators' rendering of "it could have been sold for *more than a year's wages*" fits very well. The onlookers obviously considered the worth of the perfume to be a large amount.

But the larger sums come when there is reference to minas or talents. Both are designations of weight, useable for weighing commodities such as grain, as well as for weighing out precious metal. Because of the size involved, it is unlikely that minas or talents were ever minted into coinage but rather were weighed out in smaller pieces to arrive at a total value.

The only place in the New Testament where minas are mentioned is in Luke chapter 19. There Jesus says, "A man of noble birth went to a distant country to have himself appointed king and then to return. So he called ten of his servants and gave them ten minas. 'Put this money to work,' he said, 'until I come back'" (verses 12,13).

In this parable a nobleman parcels out a mina to each of ten servants. A mina is calculated to have weighed 0.6 kilograms, about a pound and a quarter, or 20 ounces. We're not told whether the minas were of silver or gold. At the time of this writing, the spot price of silver is $16.55; gold is $1,005.70. Let's assume the minas given out were in gold. Twenty ounces would be worth $20,114.00. That's not exactly chump change.

But the bigger money comes when dealing in talents:

"Therefore, the kingdom of heaven is like a king who wanted to settle accounts with his servants. As he began the settlement, a man who owed him ten thousand talents was brought to him. Since he was not able to pay, the master ordered that he and his wife and his children and all that he had be sold to repay the debt.

"The servant fell on his knees before him. 'Be patient with me,' he begged, 'and I will pay back everything.' The servant's master took pity on him, canceled the debt and let him go.

"But when that servant went out, he found one of his fellow servants who owed him a hundred denarii. He grabbed him and began to choke him. 'Pay back what you owe me!' he demanded.

"His fellow servant fell to his knees and begged him, 'Be patient with me, and I will pay you back.'

"But he refused. Instead, he went off and had the man thrown into prison until he could pay the debt." (Matthew 18:23-30)

As mentioned previously, a talent also was a measure of weight—in this case, a weight of about 75 pounds. Assuming the parable is speaking of silver talents, 75 pounds of silver at $16.55 an ounce would make each talent worth in the vicinity of $1,241.00. Debtor A's obligation of 10,000 talents was obviously off the charts, a totally impossible debt to repay. On the other hand, the 100 denarii owed by debtor B, less than a half year's wages, could readily have been repaid. The enormous debt owed by debtor A serves admirably to impress on us the huge debt that a gracious God has forgiven all of us. Dare we do any less in dealing with the small-time "debtors" who occasionally come into our lives?

Small Coins

As noted previously, while their country was occupied by Roman soldiers, the Jews were not permitted to mint their own precious metal coins. But they could mint small coins using nonprecious metals, coins of bronze or copper. The generic term for these small coins was *lepta*. That term is derived from a Greek adjective meaning "small" or "thin." The account of the widow casting into the temple treasury her two "mites," as they have popularly come to be called, gives us the specific name of one category of small coins:

> Jesus sat down opposite the place where the offerings were put and watched the crowd putting their money into the temple treasury. Many rich people threw in large amounts. But a poor widow came and put in two very small copper coins, worth only a fraction of a penny.
>
> Calling his disciples to him, Jesus said, "I tell you the truth, this poor widow has put more into the treasury than all the others." (Mark 12:41-43)

Literally the text says she put in "two *lepta*, which equals a *kodrant*." Just as we have a coin we refer to as a quarter, so did the Jews. Their quarter (which is what *kodrant* means) was one fourth of an *assarion*, which in turn was one sixteenth of a *denarius*.

Realizing how difficult it is to assign specific values to early coinage, we can appreciate the translators' difficulty in finding meaningful equivalents for terms like *lepta* and *kodrants*. That in turn makes us more receptive to the NIV's interpretation: that the widow gave "two very small copper coins, worth only a fraction of a penny."

We need to remind ourselves that the Holy Spirit's point in recording this incident is not to determine the monetary value of the widow's gift, but rather to teach us the enduring truth that it is not quantity that makes a gift acceptable. It is the trust and love toward our Savior-God that motives the gift. That ennobles even small gifts.

Value-Neutral Coins

In the previous two sections, we have dealt with money denominations that were either very large or very small. In some New Testament passages, the value of the money involved is incidental to the situation described. What is more important in those cases is the coin's nationality, that is, the country where the coin originated. We have such an incident when Jesus deals with his Jewish enemies. They are tying to trick him into giving an answer that will either make him look like a Roman sympathizer for paying taxes or like a disloyal tax evader for refusing to pay:

> *Then the Pharisees went out and laid plans to trap him in his words. They sent their disciples to him along with the Herodians. "Teacher," they said, "we know you are a man of integrity and that you teach the way of God in accordance with the truth. You aren't swayed by men, because you pay no attention to who they are. Tell us then, what is your opinion? Is it right to pay taxes to Caesar or not?"*
>
> *But Jesus, knowing their evil intent, said, "You hypocrites, why are you trying to trap me? Show me the coin used for paying the tax." They brought him a denarius, and he asked them, "Whose portrait is this? And whose inscription?"*
>
> *"Caesar's," they replied.*
>
> *Then he said to them, "Give to Caesar what is Caesar's, and to God what is God's."* (Matthew 22:15-21)

Here the value of the coin is incidental. The important aspect is that the denarius was a coin issued by the Roman government. Jesus' enemies tried to trick him into giving an "either/or" answer. Jesus informs them that it is rather a "both/and" situation. Obviously they should fulfill their obligation to God, but if they are willing to use the denarius—the coin of the realm featuring a picture of the emperor Tiberius on the front and an official inscription on the reverse side—then they are obligated also to respect the Roman government.

In his gospel, Matthew, a former tax collector, includes an incident that involves another tax coin. Here it is in reference to an Old Testament tax that came to be known as the temple tax. Although the Old Testament speaks of this tax as requiring the payment of a half *shekel*, Matthew uses terms for Greek coins, the *drachma* and the *stater*:

> *After Jesus and his disciples arrived in Capernaum, the collectors of the two-drachma tax came to Peter and asked, "Doesn't your teacher pay the temple tax?"*
>
> *"Yes, he does," he replied.*

> *When Peter came into the house, Jesus was the first to speak. "What do you think, Simon?" he asked. "From whom do the kings of the earth collect duty and taxes—from their own sons or from others?"*
>
> *"From others," Peter answered.*
>
> *"Then the sons are exempt," Jesus said to him. "But so that we may not offend them, go to the lake and throw out your line. Take the first fish you catch; open its mouth and you will find a four-drachma coin. Take it and give it to them for my tax and yours."* (Matthew 17:24-27)

The term *drachma* derives from a Greek word meaning "a handful," though a handful of what remains something of a mystery. A suggested answer is that it refers to a handful of the small iron rings, bars, or rods that continued to be used in some Greek areas even after precious metal coins came into vogue. At Jesus' time the drachma circulated as a silver coin. Apparently the "two-drachma" that the tax collector questioned Peter about equaled the half shekel required for the temple tax. Matthew calls the coin that came in the mouth of Peter's fish a *stater*, another silver coin of Greek background that had been absorbed into the Jewish monetary system. Equal to four drachmas, a stater was adequate to pay the temple tax for both Jesus and Peter.

We are not told whether Peter had to get the stater changed into half shekels, though there certainly were money changers present to render such service. These money changers were a mixed blessing. They made available the required coin for worshipers to pay their temple tax. Unfortunately, however, they were often dishonest, offering poor exchange rates and padding their commissions. They were often so corrupt that Jesus accuses them of changing his Father's house of prayer into a "den of robbers" (Matthew 21:13). Together with the sellers of sacrificial animals, they formed a serious distraction to worship life in the temple. It's no wonder Jesus began and closed his public ministry with a cleansing of the temple.

Why didn't out-of-town pilgrims go to the local bank to get their money changed? Answer: Because banks as we know them were rare in those days, though not entirely unknown. In Old Testament times, there were clear regulations against charging interest on money loaned to a poor brother. In New Testament times, however, those restrictions seem to have fallen away. The parable of the rich man giving out talents to his servants yields some helpful insights, particularly in connection with the owner's reproach to the lazy servant who made no money for his master with the one talent entrusted to him:

> *"Then the man who had received the one talent came. 'Master,' he said, 'I knew that you are a hard man, harvesting where you have not sown and gathering where you have not scattered seed. So I was afraid and went out and hid your talent in the ground. See, here is what belongs to you.'*
>
> *"His master replied, 'You wicked, lazy servant! So you knew that I harvest where I have not sown and gather where I have not scattered seed? Well then, you should have put my money on deposit with the bankers, so that when I returned I would have received it back with interest.*
>
> *"'Take the talent from him and give it to the one who has the ten talents.'"* (Matthew 25:24-28)

Loaning money on interest seems to have become a standard practice. By the years A.D. 66–70 (during the Jewish rebellion against Rome), there was a separate building in Jerusalem designated specifically for housing the records of outstanding loans. We know this because the Jewish historian Josephus tells of a band of radicals who burned down this building and thus "cancelled" their debts (*The Jewish War II*, 17.6). So, loaning money to make money was a common practice in New Testament times.

The alternative to lending money to earn interest was the lazy steward's approach to wealth preservation. He buried his talent. If a rich man secretly buried his treasure and later developed Alzheimer's disease, then the stage is set for the likes of what forms the story line in one of Jesus' parables:

> *"The kingdom of heaven is like treasure hidden in a field. When a man found it, he hid it again, and then in his joy went and sold all he had and bought that field."* (Matthew 13:44)

59

Right next to the parable about treasure hidden in a field stands another parable, this one illustrating a method of converting one's holdings into portable wealth:

> *"Again, the kingdom of heaven is like a merchant looking for fine pearls. When he found one of great value, he went away and sold everything he had and bought it."* (Matthew 13:45,46)

In some ancient cultures, pearls were considered the top level of precious stones, if a pearl may be called a "stone." There is evidence that in certain places pearls were considered more valuable than gold. But pearls were not the only form of portable wealth. Clearly the ancients were acquainted with the whole range of precious and semi-precious stones, as is illustrated by the apostle John's description of the new Jerusalem:

> *The wall was made of jasper, and the city of pure gold, as pure as glass. The foundations of the city walls were decorated with every kind of precious stone. The first foundation was jasper, the second sapphire, the third chalcedony, the fourth emerald, the fifth sardonyx, the sixth carnelian, the seventh chrysolite, the eighth beryl, the ninth topaz, the tenth chrysoprase, the eleventh jacinth, and the twelfth amethyst. The twelve gates were twelve pearls, each gate made of a single pearl.* (Revelation 21:18-21)

There has been some discussion as to exactly what stones are included under the names John records. For example, in some cases opals and agates may have been included in the Greek term *margaritas*, usually rendered as "pearl."

The ancients used a number of procedures to change rough stones into gems. There was the practice of polishing stones to highlight their color and figure but to leave them in their natural shape. Carving changed the outline and edges of stones. It involved more work but yielded interesting designs, often of animals or birds. Engraving was by far the most time-consuming procedure and demanded the greatest amount of skill. Many examples of this skill have been preserved in the cylinder seals that archaeology has recovered. (Faceted stones, incidentally, did not come into vogue until the 14th century.)

There has been previous reference to the archaeological digs in which Wisconsin Lutheran Seminary at one time participated with the University of Tel Aviv in Israel. Removing the fill that has come to cover ancient sites is decidedly slow business. It involves the careful removal of cubic yards of dirt, often without finding anything of value for days on end. A significant find is cause for rejoicing. In two summers of digging, my "red-letter day" came with uncovering a small garnet seal. It was about three quarters of an inch in height, conical in shape, and beautifully incised with the picture of a mythical figure—something like a winged lion. It likely was someone's personal seal, used for signing documents or sealing packets. (For the record: Archaeologically found artifacts remain the property of the host country.)

The point to note is simply that the people of the New Testament had a knowledge of and an appreciation for the whole range of gemstones. They could picture for themselves the jasper in the walls, the 12 stones decorating the foundations, and the gates made of pearl. Without such knowledge there would have been no point of comparison to illustrate what beauty and opulence mark the new Jerusalem John is trying to describe for his readers.

3
TRAVEL AND TRANSPORT

Travel on Foot

We went on ahead to the ship and sailed for Assos, where we were going to take Paul aboard. He had made this arrangement because he was going there on foot. (Acts 20:13)

When Luke says that *"we* went on ahead to the ship," he is including the group of delegates chosen by the Gentile congregations to accompany Paul when their gift was delivered to the needy Jewish Christians in Jerusalem. The group assembled at Troas (ancient Troy), where Paul and the group spent seven days. On the final evening of their stay, Paul's farewell sermon went on until after midnight. In fact, Paul outlasted a young man named Eutychus, who fell asleep and tumbled out of a third-story window. However, Paul restored him and went back up to finish the service.

Instead of boarding ship the next morning, Paul decided to walk the 20 miles to the next city. Meanwhile, the ship would be sailing around the Cape of Lectum to pick him up at the port city of Assos. Luke gives no indication why Paul chose to walk. Perhaps it was to reflect on the events of the previous day or to brace himself for the trying times he knew awaited him in Jerusalem. Perhaps it was so he could say farewell to some special believer in the area.

The point is, Paul thought nothing of walking the 20 miles. Everyone in Palestine, and in the Mediterranean world in general, walked as a matter of course. It was virtually the only way to get anywhere. Palestine is not a particularly large country—about 125 miles "from Dan to Beersheba," that is, from north to south. Pious Jews regularly made the pilgrimage to Jerusalem located in the south central part of the country.

When Jesus sent out the Twelve on a preaching tour, he gave them clear instructions to stay in Jewish territory and not to venture into any Samaritan towns at this time. Confined to Jewish territory, the assignment obviously was a walking tour. Matthew, Mark, and

Luke all give a careful listing of things they were—or rather were *not*—to take on their tour. The following three texts are all cited because slight differences in the accounts have prompted some discussion over the ages.

Matthew 10:5-10:

⁵These twelve Jesus sent out with the following instructions: "Do not go among the Gentiles or enter any town of the Samaritans. ⁶Go rather to the lost sheep of Israel. ⁷As you go, preach this message: 'The kingdom of heaven is near.' ⁸Heal the sick, raise the dead, cleanse those who have leprosy, drive out demons. Freely you have received, freely give. ⁹Do not take along any gold or silver or copper in your belts; ¹⁰take no bag for the journey, or extra tunic, or sandals or a staff; for the worker is worth his keep."

Mark 6:7-9:

⁷Calling the Twelve to him, he sent them out two by two and gave them authority over evil spirits.

⁸These were his instructions: "Take nothing for the journey except a staff—no bread, no bag, no money in your belts. ⁹Wear sandals but not an extra tunic."

Luke 9:1-3:

¹When Jesus had called the Twelve together, he gave them power and authority to drive out all demons and to cure diseases, ²and he sent them out to preach the kingdom of God and to heal the sick. ³He told them: "Take nothing for the journey—no staff, no bag, no bread, no money, no extra tunic."

First of all, it should be noted that the verb Matthew uses at 10:9, which the NIV translates as "Do not take along . . ." is not the same as the verb in Mark 6:8 and Luke 9:3. The verb Matthew uses literally means "to acquire." Hence Jesus' directive essentially says, "Don't go out and lay in a supply of." The verb Mark and Luke use literally means "to carry." That is well reflected in the translation, "Do not take for the journey . . ."

Note that Matthew, the money man (ex-tax collector), is the only one to enumerate the three categories of coins. Gold and silver were serious money; copper was small change. All three evangelists speak of not putting money into a belt. This belt was a sash, often highly decorated, that was cinched around the waist to tie up the long flowing tunic. Usually tunics had no pockets, but small objects could be tucked into the sash so that it served as a type of wallet.

All three gospel accounts speak of not taking a "bag." Strangely, some interpreters have seen this as a beggar's bag. That interpretation seems unlikely in view of the fact that the bag is specifically said to be "for the journey." It was more likely to be in the nature of a backpack or a knapsack. As such it would be a very logical receptacle for some food or a change of clothes. Since, however, the disciples are asked not to take along food or articles of clothing, there's no need for the bag either.

Also, all three accounts say literally not to take "two" tunics. Apparently, the normal procedure would have been to carry a tunic in a knapsack so that the traveler actually would have two tunics: one on his back and another in his bag. Hence the translation "don't take an *extra* tunic" fits the situation very well.

Is there a problem with the staff? Mark 6:8 says, "Take nothing for the journey except a staff." Matthew appears to say the opposite. Here too, "don't take an extra staff" could be a possible understanding. But this suggests the awkward picture of a disciple carrying two staffs. However, if we key off the basic meaning of Matthew's choice of verb, the Lord's instruction would then be: "Don't go out to get a new staff. Use what you have."

But what about the sandals? Mark says plainly, "Wear sandals," whereas Matthew could be understood as urging them to go barefoot. Over the centuries both views have been debated and defended. The result has been the formation of monastic orders that have distinguished themselves by their footwear. Such orders remain to the present day. The 2009 Web page of the Carmelite Monks of Wyoming, residing in a monastery at the foot of the Rocky Mountains in northern Wyoming, offers an instructive example:

> Ss. John of the Cross and Teresa of Avila when instituting the Discalced Reform of Carmel in the sixteenth century, prescribed a return to the poverty of the original hermits on Mount Carmel. This poverty was manifested in many ways, but one of the best-known ways was that the Discalced

Carmelites did not wear shoes. The word "discalced" actually means "barefooted" or "shoeless." Although originally the Discalced Fathers did not wear shoes and went barefoot, St. Teresa of Jesus moderated their austerity by urging them to wear poor sandals. This has remained the custom up to present times. (www.carmelitemonks.org)

Paradoxically, making a list of all the things the Twelve were not to carry as "extras" gives us a pretty good idea as to what a traveler would normally have taken for a journey. There was the indispensable tunic, the knee-length flowing garment, often sleeved but pocketless, worn next to the skin. This was held in by a belt that served also as a wallet. A knapsack held food and a change of clothes. Sturdy sandals and a stout walking stick helped him negotiate the improvised paths and rough roads he had to traverse. Two rather common items are not included in Jesus' instruction for the Twelve. There is no mention of a turbanlike covering for the head, nor any mention of a *himation*, the equivalent of a coat or jacket to go over the basic tunic. Yes, men wore skirts in New Testament times. Trousers came into vogue later, largely an import from the Persians.

Riding

Virtually every Christmas card featuring the holy family heading to Bethlehem has Mary riding on a donkey. That may well have been the case, but we have no scriptural corroboration of that detail. Actually, riding was not a very common mode of transportation. Scripture mentions Jesus riding into Jerusalem on Palm Sunday, but that was to fulfill prophecy rather than to provide distance transportation. There is, however, one instance in the New Testament Scriptures that documents travel by riding:

The commander dismissed the young man and cautioned him, "Don't tell anyone that you have reported this to me."

Then he called two of his centurions and ordered them, "Get ready a detachment of two hundred soldiers, seventy horsemen and two hundred spearmen to go to Caesarea at nine tonight. Provide mounts for Paul so that he may be taken safely to Governor Felix." (Acts 23:22-24)

Recall the circumstances underlying the incident cited above. Paul's nephew (Acts 23:16) had overheard information about a Jewish plot to kill Paul, and he reported it to the Roman authorities. Paul was being held in Jerusalem, so the Roman commander decided to move Paul under heavy guard to the provincial capital of Caesarea, some 50 miles away. For speed and safety the commander provided Paul with "mounts."

The word translated "mounts" is as ambiguous in Greek as it is in English. It simply refers to a domesticated animal, with no indication as to whether it's a horse, a donkey, or even a camel. Nor is there any ready answer as to why the term regularly is used in the plural. The most likely assumption here is that Paul is riding horseback. There were, after all, 70 horsemen in the detail the commander assigned to this mission.

Assuming Paul's travel on this occasion was by horse also squares with the observation that horses were generally associated with the military, not privately owned. Palestine, under Roman occupation in New Testament times, obviously had no cavalry. However, one is reminded of the glory days when Solomon matched neighboring nations in amassing horses and chariots. The author of 2 Chronicles reports, "Solomon had four thousand stalls for horses and chariots, and twelve thousand horses, which he kept in the chariot cities and also with him in Jerusalem" (9:25).

Roads

With only such marginal infrastructure as trails, paths, and roads randomly developed by foot travel, what sort of distances could be covered in a day's travel? J. Kelso ventures an estimate when he writes:

> Travel was slow, for both men and animals walked; the length of the day's march depended upon the urgency of the trip. . . . Average travel for men would be about fifteen miles a day. Donkey caravans tried to make twenty miles a

day. The ordinary camel caravan of freight, with each animal carrying between 500 and 600 pounds, traveled approximately three miles an hour on a six hour day. A swift dromedary, on the other hand, could carry a rider on long journeys at seventy miles a day. (*Zondervan Pictorial Encyclopedia of the Bible*, s.v. "travel")

The daunting desert due east of Palestine, lying beyond the Jordan River, was virtually impassable. Travel routes went around it on the north in a horseshoe-shaped pattern. This course followed a fairly narrow strip of arable land that has come to be called the Fertile Crescent. It stretched from Egypt to Mesopotamia (modern Iraq). Palestine lay at the southwestern end of this crescent.

With its north-south orientation, Palestine was served by two international roads. One was called the Way of the Sea *(Via Maris)*, which originated in the Suez region of Egypt and entered Palestine at Gaza. From there it proceeded along the coast of the Mediterranean up to the Plain of Sharon, where it bent inland to pass through Galilee and on to Damascus to join with a major east-west road continuing on to Mesopotamia.

A second international road, called the King's Highway, started from the Gulf of Elath on the Red Sea and proceeded to the north on the east side of the Jordan River, thus also reaching Damascus and joining the east-west trunk road.

A major step in connecting Europe to this essentially Asiatic trade route was Rome's development of an excellent system of paved roads. In fact, few things reveal more clearly the Roman "can do" attitude than their skill and dedication to road building. It is reported that at one time Rome had 29 military roads radiating out from the capital. Many of these extended out to become major international roads. A case in point is the Egnatian Highway *(Via Egnatia)* on which the apostle Paul surely traveled. Its first major stop outside of Rome was at the city of Dyrrhachium (Durres in modern Albania). From there it extended eastward as far as Thessalonica, where the traveler could continue on to the east and follow the Fertile Crescent or could head north to Byzantium (modern Istanbul).

Life in the New Testament World

Roman roads were so well engineered and solidly constructed that in many places they remain intact today. The Web site for United Nations of Roma Victrix (UNRV; www.unrv.com/culture/roman-road-construction.php), in speaking of the Roman Empire, describes the road-building technique generally in use:

> Standard Roman roads consisted of a metalled surface (i.e. gravel or pebbles) on a solid foundation of earth or stone.
>
> A simple yet technologically advanced plan was in place and implemented for the construction of each road.
>
> Where possible, roads were built in the straightest line possible, only avoiding major terrain obstacles where it made practical sense. A Roman road was a multi-layered architectural achievement, but the construction process was fairly simple to define.
>
> First the two parallel trenches were built on either side of the planned road, with the resulting earthworks, stone, etc., being dumped and built up in the space between the two ditches. The Agger, as this was called, could be up to 6 ft. (1.8 m) high and 50 ft. (15 m) wide. Alternatively it could be very slight or almost non-existent as was the case with most minor roads.
>
> Next, the diggers would make a shallow 8 to 10 foot wide depression down the length of the agger, and line the edges with kerb (curb) stones to hold the entire construction in place. The bottom of this depression would then be lined with a series of stone fillers. 6 to 8 inch stones would form the foundation layer, with fist sized stones placed on top. In early roads the remaining gap would then be filled in with course [sic] sand to fill between the stones and to cover them by approximately 1 ft.
>
> Later roads may have used Roman volcanic concrete to mix the entire mixture together making the whole structure more solid. The road surface was then laid down using large, tight fitting, flat stones that could be found and transported locally. These larger surface stones would be

cut to fit when possible to make the surface as smooth and seamless as possible.

The roads were built by the army and intended for military purposes—mainly to control conquered nations by supplying garrisons and setting up checkpoints. But they also generated revenue for Rome through toll fees and tariffs on goods in transit. (Remember Matthew, the tax collector, sitting in his tax booth beside the road.) Although the roads were made by and for the military, the Romans did not prevent anyone from using them. This was a boon not only for walking travelers, but it proved to be a real blessing for businessmen who could now move much greater quantities of goods by loading things into wheeled vehicles that became more practical with better roads.

Although written for a far different purpose than to give us a list of the goods and commodities that moved through the transportation systems in New Testament times, the apostle John's account in Revelation chapter 18 can serve in that way. There John describes the commercial dislocation caused by wicked "Babylon's" fall. John lists an impressive number of goods that will no longer be marketed. John's readers must have known about such goods being in transit. John writes:

"The merchants of the earth will weep and mourn over her [Babylon] because no one buys their cargoes any more—cargoes of gold, silver, precious stones and pearls; fine linen, purple, silk and scarlet cloth; every sort of citron wood, and articles of every kind made of ivory, costly wood, bronze, iron and marble; cargoes of cinnamon and spice, of incense, myrrh and frankincense, of wine and olive oil, of fine flour and wheat; cattle and sheep; horses and carriages; and bodies and souls of men." (Revelation 18:11-13)

High on the list of benefits was the communication link that roads provided. Here too it was primarily the military that needed a communication system so as to stay in touch with the outlying providences. But it was a resource soon capitalized on for gospel outreach. The apostles, sent out to the four corners of the inhabited world, could travel almost anywhere in relative safety. It is a blessing noted by the second-century church father Irenaeus in his book *Against Heresies:* "The Romans have given the world peace, and we travel without fear along the roads and cross the seas wherever we wish" (iv, 30, 3).

With 29 roads radiating out of Rome, it was not much of an exaggeration for proud Romans to assert, "All roads lead to Rome." But with all the benefits and advantages a good road system brought for the empire, it also introduced one serious flaw. It created a situation in which it was just as easy for marauding bands and hostile nations to march into the city of Rome as it was for Roman troops to rush out and quell some distant uprising.

Travel by Water

SEA OF GALILEE

The observation is often made that the Jewish nation was not a seafaring people. Solomon had a navy, but with no good harbors on the Mediterranean coast, it was based on the Red Sea. It was built in cooperation with Hiram of Tyre and operated with considerable help from his Phoenician sailors. We read in I Kings: "King Solomon also built ships at Ezion Geber, which is near Elath in Edom, on the shore of the Red Sea. And Hiram sent his men—sailors who knew the sea—to serve in the fleet with Solomon's men" (9:26,27).

Under Roman domination the Jewish nation had no navy, either military or commercial. Their participation in water travel was largely confined to the Lake of Galilee.

In Old Testament times, this inland body of freshwater was known as Lake Chinnereth. The name means "harp," chosen because its shoreline resembles the outline of a harp. In the gospels it is referred to as the Sea of Galilee, the Sea of Tiberias, Lake Genneserat, or simply the Sea. Much of Jesus' ministry was conducted around, or even *on*, this body of water. Mark records one dramatic incident:

> *Immediately [after the feeding of the five thousand] Jesus made his disciples get into the boat and go on ahead of him to Bethsaida, while*

he dismissed the crowd. After leaving them, he went up on a mountainside to pray.

When evening came, the boat was in the middle of the lake, and he was alone on land. He saw the disciples straining at the oars, because the wind was against them. About the fourth watch of the night he went out to them, walking on the lake. (Mark 6:45-48)

When they saw that Jesus could miraculously feed thousands of people, the people wanted to make Jesus a "bread king." To forestall such a perversion of his spiritual mission on earth, Jesus dismissed the crowd and had his disciples take their boat back to the little fishing village of Bethsaida. He, meanwhile, retired to a mountain to pray.

From his mountain retreat, Jesus saw the Twelve "straining at the oars"—which incidentally supports the assumption that rowing was a common means of propulsion on the Sea of Galilee. But what kind of boat would the Twelve have been rowing? By good fortune a wooden rowboat has been discovered that can be dated to New Testament times.

In 1986, at a time of very low water in the lake, two brothers, fishermen themselves, discovered what appeared to be the remains of a wooden boat submerged in the mud. Careful archaeological removal proved the brothers' hunch to be correct. Radiocarbon dating served as the basis for estimating that the craft dates back to 40 B.C., plus or minus 80 years. Through careful preservation procedures, the boat has been stabilized so as to allow it to be put on display for the public. Its dimension are a little over 26 feet long, $7^1/_2$ feet wide, and about 4 feet high—big enough to accommodate 12 sturdy rowers.

But despite the efforts of a dozen rowers, Jesus' disciples weren't getting anywhere because "the wind was against them." Adverse winds on the lake are not at all unusual. Because of the topography of the area, sudden storms can come up at any time.

The Sea of Galilee lies in what geologists call the Great Rift Valley. It's a huge crack in the earth beginning in Syria, extending down the Jordan Valley though the Dead Sea, on into the Red Sea, and even into Africa as far south as Victoria Falls on the Zambezi River.

The surface of the Sea of Galilee lies at about 685 feet below sea level, so its climate is tropical. The lake has a north-south orientation, with the Jordan River flowing through it from the north. It has a maximum depth of about 140 feet. On both the east and west sides of the lake, steep cliffs rise about 2,600 feet above the water. Cold air masses drifting in from the Mediterranean or sliding down from snowcapped Mount Hermon can easily clash with the warm tropical air at lake level. The result is sudden and violent storms posing great danger to small crafts. (See Matthew 8:24.)

Mark tells us that when Jesus observed the disciples struggling in the storm, "the boat was in the middle of the lake." How far the middle is from shore obviously depends on the size of the lake. Depending on where the measurements are taken, the lake is approximately 13 miles long and 8 miles wide. Even if the disciples crossed at the widest point (which is unlikely seeing they were heading toward Bethsaida on the north shore), they would have been about 4 miles out on the lake.

The evangelist John's account in John 6:19 corroborates that approximate distance with an expression the translators have rendered as "three or three and a half miles." Literally John says, "When they had rowed 25 or 30 *stadia* . . ." A *stadion* equals about 600 feet. Related to our word *stadium*, a *stadion* was a term from athletics. The racers would start from "scratch," run downfield and round a pillar 100 yards away, and then return to the scratch (now the finish) line. Incidentally, local jocks often referred to this event as the "hairpin" because of the bobby pin–like configuration of the track it was run on. Be that as it may, 100 yards going and another 100 yards returning yields the 600 feet mentioned above. Do the math on "25 or 30 stadia," and it becomes evident that the interpretive rendering of "three or three and a half miles" is a very workable conversion to our units of measure.

In this incident we also get a glimpse into the prayer life of our Savior. It was evening when Jesus dismissed the crowd and sent off his disciples by boat. He later appeared to them "about the fourth watch." In New Testament times, the night was divided into four three-hour watches: 6:00–9:00 P.M., 9:00 P.M.–12:00 A.M., 12:00–3:00 A.M., and 3:00–6:00 A.M. If the disciples were sent off at about

8:00 P.M. and Jesus appeared to them on the water at about 4:00 A.M., we have eight hours of private time between Jesus and his heavenly Father. Granted, our circumstances are very different, but Jesus' example does pose to each of us the searching question: How much private time per day are we spending with our heavenly Father?

Oceangoing Travel

As noted previously, the Jewish nation was not much inclined to take to the sea. Just as they depended on their neighbors to supply them with gold and silver coins, so they depended on their neighbors to provide sea transportation for people and goods. The most adept sailors in New Testament times were the Phoenicians, who were based just north of Palestine in the cities of Tyre and Sidon.

Oceangoing ships came in different sizes, of course, but there were basically two types: smaller vessels that hopped from port to port, staying within sight of land, and larger craft that headed out on the high seas. As for size, archaeologists have discovered a dry dock that is 130 feet long. Ancient authors tell of ships as long as 180 feet and of vessels carrying as many as six hundred people. Virtually all oceangoing vessels were sailboats, though some had the capability of adding oar power should the ship be caught on a calm sea. Large stern oars served as rudders to aid in navigation.

Although it's decidedly pre–New Testament times, Ezekiel's divinely inspired denunciation of Tyre offers an instructive picture of Tyrian shipping:

> *The word of the LORD came to me: "Son of man, take up a lament concerning Tyre. Say to Tyre, situated at the gateway to the sea, merchant of peoples on many coasts, 'This is what the Sovereign LORD says:*
>
> *"'You say, O Tyre, "I am perfect in beauty." Your domain was on the high seas; your builders brought your beauty to perfection. They made all your timbers of pine trees from Senir; they took a cedar from Lebanon to make a mast for you. Of oaks from Bashan they made your oars; of cypress wood from the coasts of Cyprus they made your deck, inlaid with ivory. Fine embroidered linen from Egypt was your sail and served as your banner; your awnings were of blue and purple from the coasts of Elishah. Men of Sidon and Arvad were your oarsmen; your skilled men, O Tyre, were aboard as your seamen. Veteran*

craftsmen of Gebal were on board as shipwrights to caulk your seams. All the ships of the sea and their sailors came alongside to trade for your wares.'" (Ezekiel 27:1-9)

Then there follows (verses 10-24) a list of some 20 nations doing business with Tyre. Included among them are Persia (Mesopotamia), Lydia (Asia Minor), Put (Africa), Greece (eastern Europe), and Tarshish (western Europe). Of special interest is the notice in verse 17 of Jewish commercial activity, "Judah and Israel traded with you; they exchanged wheat from Minnith and confections, honey, oil and balm for your wares."

Speaking directly to Tyre, Ezekiel delivers God's dread warning about destruction to come:

"'You are filled with heavy cargo in the heart of the sea. Your oarsmen take you out to the high seas. But the east wind will break you to pieces in the heart of the sea. Your wealth, merchandise and wares, your mariners, seamen and shipwrights, your merchants and all your soldiers, and everyone else on board will sink into the heart of the sea on the day of your shipwreck.'" (Ezekiel 27:25b-27)

Ezekiel's words were not an empty threat. Considerable work has been done to examine the remains of Tyre's harbor with its elaborate system of stone docks and piers. But it's different from the ordinary type of archaeology. Here everything is underwater, mute testimony that God will not be mocked by an arrogant nation.

As a record of sea travel during New Testament times, Luke's account of the apostle Paul's travel to Jerusalem on the return portion of his third missionary journey gives us a look at both types of ocean travel: short hops and longer voyages.

There is reference first of all to the smaller port-hopping type of vessel "coasting" along the Asia Minor shore of the Aegean Sea. On the return from his third missionary journey, Paul was being accompanied by a delegation from the European Gentile congregations that were delivering a gift to the needy Jewish believers in Jerusalem. The group assembled at Troas and took shipping to the next port city of Assos. Recall, however, that Paul chose to walk to Assos, where he was to be picked up by the ship that would be stopping at numerous ports on its run along the Asia Minor coast.

Travel and Transport

Luke, always careful with details, enumerates the various stops at the end of each travel day. Picking up the story with Paul's arrival at Assos, Luke reports:

> *When [Paul] met us at Assos, we took him aboard and went on to Mitylene [capital of the island of Lesbos]. The next day we set sail from there and arrived off Kios [an island]. The day after that we crossed over to Samos [island], and on the following day arrived at Miletus [an Asia Minor mainland port]. Paul had decided to sail past Ephesus to avoid spending time in the province of Asia, for he was in a hurry to reach Jerusalem, if possible, by the day of Pentecost.* (Acts 20:14-16)

From Miletus, Paul sent word to the church leaders in Ephesus, asking them to come the 36 miles to Miletus. After describing the painful task of taking leave of these elders, among whom he had spent three years of ministry—the longest of Paul's stays recorded in Acts—Luke continues:

> *After we [Paul's party] had torn ourselves away from them [the Ephesian elders], we put out to sea and sailed straight to Cos [an island]. The next day we went to Rhodes [an island] and from there to Patara [a mainland port].* (Acts 21:1)

Apparently Patara, a city at the southwestern corner of Asia Minor, was the end of the line for the midsized vessel Paul and his party had utilized so far. No doubt this ship turned around and port hopped its way back to Troas and even beyond to Macedonian and Greek ports along the northern and western shores of the Aegean Sea.

Leaving the relatively calm and protected waters of the Aegean Sea and Asia Minor coastline and venturing out on the Mediterranean Sea proper meant locating another type of vessel. What Paul and his party needed at Patara was a ship large enough to allow them to continue their journey on the next leg, namely over the Mediterranean Sea to the Phoenician/Palestinian coast.

> *We found a ship crossing over to Phoenicia, went on board and set sail. After sighting Cyprus and passing to the south of it, we sailed on to Syria. We landed at Tyre, where our ship was to unload its*

> *cargo. Finding the disciples there, we stayed with them seven days.* (Acts 21:2-4)

There was no such thing as passenger service or tickets reserving space for passengers. Paul's party "found" a ship headed for Tyre—a freighter, we're informed, carrying cargo for Tyre.

After seven days "we continued our voyage from Tyre," Luke writes in verse 7. Whether the freighter stayed in port for seven days and then continued on down the Phoenician coast or whether it returned to Patara and Paul took another smaller ship plying up and down the eastern Mediterranean coast is not told to us.

> *Finding the disciples [in Tyre], we stayed with them seven days. . . . But when our time was up, we left and continued on our way. . . . After saying good-by to each other, we went aboard the ship, and [the Christian disciples] returned home.*
>
> *We continued our voyage from Tyre and landed at Ptolemais [modern Acco], where we greeted the brothers and stayed with them for a day. Leaving the next day, we reached Caesarea and stayed at the house of Philip the evangelist, one of the Seven.* (Acts 21:4-8)

From Caesarea to Jerusalem it was necessary to travel over land—about 60 miles on foot.

If we fast-forward about two years after Paul's arrival in Caesarea at the conclusion of his third missionary journey, we find him again making a major sea trip. Upon his arrival in Jerusalem, Paul's report of very successful gospel outreach to Gentiles greatly upset the Jewish community. When it was falsely rumored that Paul had even brought Gentiles into the temple, the Jews formed a mob that was ready to lynch Paul. Humanly speaking, it was only the intervention of Roman soldiers that saved Paul's life.

But in a way, the Roman "cure" was as bad as the Jewish "disease." Once entangled in the Roman provincial legal system, Paul couldn't get out. For two years he lay in prison, waiting to have his case tried. When it became apparent that nothing was going to happen, Paul exercised his Roman citizen's right to appeal his case to Caesar. That, however, necessitated a long and arduous journey by ship to Rome:

> *When it was decided that we would sail for Italy, Paul and some other prisoners were handed over to a centurion named Julius, who belonged to the Imperial Regiment. We boarded a ship from Adramyttium about to sail for ports along the coast of the province of Asia, and we put out to sea. . . .*
>
> *The next day we landed at Sidon. . . . From there we put out to sea again and passed to the lee of Cyprus because the winds were against us. When we had sailed across the open sea off the coast of Cilicia and Pamphylia, we landed at Myra in Lycia. There the centurion found an Alexandrian ship sailing for Italy and put us on board.* (Acts 27:1-6)

It is evident that this ship was making virtually the same run as that which brought Paul to Caesarea two years earlier—only this time it was traveling in the opposite direction. Starting out from Caesarea, which was the provincial capital where Paul was being kept prisoner, this ship was scheduled to return to its home port of Adramyttium, a city in the vicinity of the previously referenced Troas and Assos. Luke tells us that en route this ship was scheduled to put in at "ports along the coast of the province of Asia [Minor]." He proceeds to enumerate reference points: Caesarea, Sidon, Cyprus, the Cilician and Pamphylian coast on the southern shore of Asia Minor, and eventually Myra.

Myra, a city in the province of Lycia at the southwestern corner of Asia Minor, was close to Patara, where Paul and his party had to change ships on their way to Jerusalem. Since Paul and his fellow travelers were not headed north toward Adramyttium but, rather, west toward Rome, they again needed to change ships here, just as on the previous journey.

It has been noted that the Phoenicians were heavily involved in the shipping trade. But by no means did they have a monopoly. Egypt was the breadbasket of the Roman Empire, and vast quantities of wheat were shipped from Alexandria to Rome. Because of treacherous sandbars off the north African coast, the Roman grain boats leaving Alexandria usually did not head directly west toward Rome but took a more northerly route. This likely is the reason why an Alexandrian ship (Alexandria was a large Egyptian port city) was in port at the Asia Minor city of Myra. Incidentally, when describing the storm that befell this ship (Acts 27:13,14,38), Luke confirms the fact that it was indeed a grain carrier Paul and his fellow travelers were on.

Although such grain freighters were often huge crafts, they were not unsinkable. In his account of Paul's ill-fated journey to Rome, Luke describes some of the dangers New Testament ships had to deal with. He refers to three natural hazards Paul's ship had to contend with: contrary winds, treacherous sandbars, and rocky coastlines.

The trip itself is best divided into three stages: the leg from mainland Palestine to the port city of Myra on the Asia Minor coast, Myra to the island of Crete, and then Crete to the shipwreck site on the island of Malta.

On the first leg of the journey, immediately upon heading out on the high seas, the ship was beset by adverse westerly winds. Sailing on the protected east side of the island of Cyprus provided some relief and allowed the ship to put into port at Myra.

Things did not improve on the second leg when they left the port of Myra and headed west:

We made slow headway for many days and had difficulty arriving off Cnidus. When the wind did not allow us to hold our course, we sailed to the lee of Crete, opposite Salmone. We moved along the coast with difficulty and came to a place called Fair Havens, near the town of Lasea. (Acts 27:7,8)

Buffeted by strong westerly winds, the ship was driven off course—far to the south of its intended route—to the leeward side of the island of Crete. The ship captain had left Myra at a risky time in the shipping season. With the frustrating delay caused by the contrary winds, things now turned decidedly ugly:

Much time had been lost, and sailing had already become dangerous because by now it was after the Fast. So Paul warned them, "Men, I can see that our voyage is going to be disastrous and bring great loss to ship and cargo, and to our own lives also." (Acts 27:9,10)

Ancient sources state that the optimum time for sailing the Mediterranean was from June to the middle of September. The two months on either side of that window were risky, and sailing in winter was an invitation to disaster. Luke supplies the information that it was now "after the Fast." His reference undoubtedly is to the Day of Atonement, which would place the time of arrival of Paul's ship at Crete sometime into October. Citing the lateness of the season, Paul urged the cautious procedure of wintering in the port of Fair Haven, but his advice was not heeded. The captain's attempt to move to a better harbor proved to be a bad mistake:

> *When a gentle south wind began to blow, they thought they had obtained what they wanted; so they weighed anchor and sailed along the shore of Crete. Before very long, a wind of hurricane force, called the "northeaster," swept down from the island. The ship was caught by the storm and could not head into the wind; so we gave way to it and were driven along.* (Acts 27:13-15)

Far off course to the south, there now was danger of being blown onto the sand shoals that make the coast off north Africa a graveyard for ships. To head off that disaster, a number of remedies were attempted:

> *As we passed to the lee of a small island called Cauda, we were hardly able to make the lifeboat secure. When the men had hoisted it aboard, they passed ropes under the ship itself to hold it together. Fearing that they would run aground on the sandbars of Syrtis, they lowered the sea anchor and let the ship be driven along.* (Acts 27:16,17)

It was common practice to pull a small boat behind, both to serve as transportation for leaving and returning to the ship when it was in port and also to serve as a lifeboat when out on the high seas.

Another measure was an attempt to secure the integrity of the ship's hull. The constant pounding of the surf could open up caulked seams and allow water to enter the ship's hold. To prevent such a dangerous development, the hull of the ship was literally trussed up with ropes to keep everything together.

A further defensive measure is more problematic to decipher. The difficult term is the Greek noun *skeuos*. It is a very common term with so generic a meaning as "thing" or "object." It can also refer to a tool or a piece of equipment. The most common meaning is "dish" or "utensil." Our translation here renders it as "sea anchor." That is assigning the word a meaning not found elsewhere, but it does make sense in the context. It would then likely be referring to something like an anchor hanging straight down in deep water, intended to catch bottom in shallow water and thus prevent the ship from drifting into the dreaded sandbars in the Mediterranean Sea, here referred to as *Syrtis*.

Others, questioning the "sea anchor" translation, have theorized that it may have involved taking down the mainsail and letting it trail behind the ship so as to cause a "drag" that would slow down the ship's southward drift toward the deadly sandbars. Regardless of which option one chooses, the measure can be deemed a success, since the ship avoided getting trapped in the sand shoals.

> *We took such a violent battering from the storm that the next day they began to throw the cargo overboard.* (Acts 27:18)

There has been repeated reference to Paul's ship as a grain freighter. Apparently, however, it also carried some other cargo. These things were now thrown overboard to lighten the ship and thus reduce the chances of it swamping:

> *On the third day, they threw the ship's tackle overboard with their own hands.* (Acts 27:19)

The word translated "tackle" confronts us with much the same problem as we saw two verses earlier. It's a parallel form to the word *skeuos* discussed in verse 17. Only here it's the feminine noun *skeue*. It's obviously a naval term adequately rendered with "tackle" or "rigging"—ropes, cables, canvas, anything loose that could be thrown overboard.

> *When neither sun nor stars appeared for many days and the storm continued raging, we finally gave up all hope of being saved.*

> *On the fourteenth night we were still being driven across the Adriatic Sea, when about midnight the sailors sensed they were approaching land. Fearing that we would be dashed against the rocks, they dropped four anchors from the stern and prayed for daylight.* (Acts 27:20,27,29)

TRAVEL AND TRANSPORT

After a harrowing two weeks of being driven across the Adriatic (a regional name for the area of the Mediterranean Sea around Italy), a break finally appeared. The sailors sensed land ahead. After they had anchored the ship in 90 feet of water (verse 28) to prevent its being driven up on a rocky shore, Paul gave the sound advice to crew and passengers to eat a hearty meal. They would need it for the shipwreck they would soon be experiencing.

When they had eaten as much as they wanted, they lightened the ship by throwing the grain into the sea. (Acts 27:38)

Previously they had jettisoned much of the incidental "cargo" the ship was carrying. On the next day, they threw the ship's "tackle" overboard. Next they resorted to the extreme measure of lightening the ship by throwing out its main cargo of grain. No doubt all 276 passengers and crew pitched in to accomplish this task.

When daylight came, they did not recognize the land, but they saw a bay with a sandy beach, where they decided to run the ship aground if they could. Cutting loose the anchors, they left them in the sea and at the same time untied the ropes that held the rudders. Then they hoisted the foresail to the wind and made for the beach. (Acts 27:39,40)

After lightening the ship by dumping its grain cargo, it made no sense to bring heavy anchors on board, so they left them in the sea. Also, the two large stern oars, lashed down during normal sailing, were loosed to provide some navigation toward the bay they had spotted. Even if the interpretation is correct that the large mainsail had been taken down to provide some drag for the ship, there would still have been the smaller foresail to provide some thrust toward shore. However, these best laid plans went awry in the storm.

But the ship struck a sandbar and ran aground. The bow stuck fast and would not move, and the stern was broken to pieces by the pounding of the surf.

. . . [Julius the centurion] ordered those who could swim to jump overboard first and get to land. The rest were to get there on planks or on pieces of the ship. In this way everyone reached land in safety. (Acts 27:41,43,44)

Luke's reference to using "planks" as flotation devices highlights an interesting aspect of travel aboard grain freighters. Large grain freighters were sometimes "decked over." Usually, however, they were "open hull," with the grain simply poured into the hold in bulk form, that is, not bagged or boxed.

But ship captains also regularly took on passengers. To provide something of a flat surface for these passengers to occupy during the trip, a temporary floor of planks was often laid out on the loose grain. That, however, was about the only amenity provided. Passengers camped out on the improvised deck in all kinds of weather. In the present case, 276 people were roughing it on the limited space available. It does not take a vivid imagination to picture the irritations and inconveniences suffered en route. Sea travel in New Testament times did not include luxury cruises!

THE ROMAN OCCUPATION OF PALESTINE: A SKETCH OF ROMAN HISTORY

Introduction

In those days Caesar Augustus issued a decree that a census should be taken of the entire Roman world. (Luke 2:1)

When Luke wrote his gospel for Theophilus, he could take many things for granted. For example, he could expect Theophilus to know who Caesar Augustus was and how he came to be the ruler of "the entire Roman world." We're far removed from that scene and likely wonder about the course of events that put one man in charge of what Luke literally calls "the entire *inhabited* world."

Rome had been around for a very long while already in New Testament times. At the point of history where Luke cuts in with his gospel account, Rome was already in the third stage of its development. Initially, Rome was a monarchy. Then it became a republic as an energized citizenry took over the government, only to lose their powers eventually to individual strongmen who grabbed for themselves the powers formerly wielded by the people. History has come to call these dictators "emperors." Caesar Augustus was the first of a long line of such absolute rulers who could fairly be said to rule over "the entire inhabited world."

Founding of the City

Obviously, the center and capital of the Roman Empire was Rome, but how did that great city get its start? We encounter many myths and legends as we try to answer that question. Much of the ancient lore is self-serving—for example, the stories trying to establish the semidivine nature of its founder Romulus. Supposedly the union of Mars, the Roman god of war, with the human priestess Rhea Silva resulted in the birth of the twins Romulus and Remus. Because of a prophecy that twins would replace the existing government, the mother was ordered to destroy her children by exposing them to the elements. Some versions of the legend speak of something like a Moses-in-the-bulrushes rescue. Others speak of a wolf taking and nursing the twins. Still others report the much more prosaic account of a shepherd named Faustulus adopting and rearing the boys.

True to the prophecy, the twins, now grown men, succeeded in forging an alliance between their home territory, that is, the Latin-speaking people of Latium, and their Sabine neighbors to the south and the Etruscans to the north.

To celebrate this consolidation of power, the brothers proposed the founding of a capital city, but they quarreled over who should have ultimate control over it. The result of the altercation was that Romulus ended up killing his brother. Now sole ruler, Romulus chose a city site where the Tiber River could be forded, built a city with impressive architecture, and declared himself king.

The Roman Monarchy

The traditional date for the founding of Rome, repeated often enough by Roman historians to become accepted, is 753 B.C. Of course, our designating it as B.C. is a modern calculation, figuring back from the time of Christ. Interestingly enough, the traditional date for the founding of Rome served for many centuries in the same way, namely, as the starting point for counting calendar years. Individual years were named after the two *consuls* (the highest governmental officials, who were elected annually) of that year, but the years were counted by starting from the founding of Rome. Thus, if we were to designate the year of Jesus' birth as 0, they would have designated it as 753 A.U.C. (753 years *ab urbe cortida*, which means "after the founding of the city"). It wasn't until the time of Charlemagne (A.D. 800) that the Christian way of numbering years became generally accepted.

The date 753 B.C. marks not only the founding of the city of Rome but also the beginning of the monarchy. Romulus was the first king. The following six kings—each chosen by the people and not by dynastic succession—served for life. In this way the monarchy is thought to have lasted until 509 B.C., thus allowing an average administration of some 35 years per king.

The seventh of those kings, a man named Tarquin, earned the dubious distinction of being branded Tarquin the Proud. So tactless and overbearing was his rule that the disenchanted populace opted not to choose a successor. Rather, they chose to keep in their own hands the power they previously had willingly ceded to the king. Thus began the era of the constitutionally regulated citizen-run government generally referred to as the Roman Republic.

The Roman Republic

The abolition of the monarchy did not lead to civil unrest. In an orderly way, the powers that the citizens had previously granted to the king were now delegated to magistrates selected from among the Roman people.

Already under the monarchy a rather complex constitution was in the process of being developed. It was unwritten, basically made up from a series of precedents. The main change that needed to be made in order to turn the new government into a republic was to parcel out the various "powers" to individuals, rather than have them all reside in the person of a king. To accomplish this division of powers, they regularly elected two persons to most of the offices. For example, they had two *consuls* (presidents or prime ministers) with equal power so that one could veto what the other was doing if he judged that the actions of his partner were not in the best interests of the republic. Also, office holders were elected to one-year terms, thus lessening the opportunity for corruption since they could be prosecuted as soon as their terms were up.

There was also a system of checks and balances among the classes living in Rome. Technically, there were four classes of people living in Rome during the republic: slaves, plebeians, knights, and patricians. Slaves had no vote and very few privileges. The knights, sometimes referred to as cavalry, were upwardly mobile and quite often became members of the patrician class. So, for all practical purposes there were two classes: plebeians and patricians.

Patricians were the landed gentry, aristocrats born into the old, established families. They figured prominently in the governance of the city. It is occasionally reported that the *senate* (highest ruling assembly) began with one hundred members from the patrician class.

The plebeian class, made up largely of farmers and merchants, was the larger of the two classes, but socially they ranked somewhat lower than the patricians. They were intelligent and ambitious people, sometimes as rich as the patricians and often inclined to be politically active. All they lacked was blue blood. It's not surprising, therefore, that they soon clamored for a share in the ruling process.

Over the years and by various strategies for applying pressure, the plebeians were able to effect changes in the constitution that gave them significant power and considerable opportunity to participate in the governing process. The greatest concession made to them was allowing them to be elected to the various executive *magistracies*—though their elections to these offices still had to be approved by the senate. Strictly speaking, the senate did not rule directly in election matters but, rather, gave "advice." The general assembly of citizens soon learned that it was not politically expedient to ignore senatorial advice. Initiatives put into law by such joint activity were often given a seal of approval by attaching to them the acronym *SPQR*, shorthand for "approved by the senate and the Roman people."

There was a wide variety of offices open to Roman citizens. In time there came into existence a succession of four offices through which the professional politician was expected to pass. Romans referred to it as the *cursus honorum* (succession of offices). Completing the lower offices successfully could put a man into the position of seeking the highest office by age 43, at the earliest. Although there were other offices outside the *cursus honorum*, the four within it were the basic senatorial offices. From lowest to highest they were: *quaestor, aedile, praetor,* and *consul.*

After completing ten years of military service, a Roman citizen at age 30 was eligible to run for one of the two quaestor positions. That office made him (together with a second quaestor) responsible for administering the public treasury and for serving as quartermaster for the huge standing army Rome had to keep to maintain control of its vast holdings throughout the world. A quaestor's term of office was for one year, and he could not seek reelection to the same office until ten years had elapsed.

At age 37 he could seek one of the two aedile offices. This office made him responsible for maintaining Rome's many temples, but it soon broadened out to make him a director of public works. He was also responsible for procuring adequate supplies of food and water for the city.

At age 40 a Roman citizen could run for the office of praetor. That position made the two holders of the office responsible for administering justice, primarily to stop corruption on the part of provincial administrators. A significant aspect of this office was that its holder was expected to pay for the entertainment that increasingly was being demanded by the people of Rome. Hence, it was a rich man's office, yet it was a prestigious one in that a praetor was attended by six *lictors* (bodyguards) when he appeared in public.

After having gained wide political and practical experience in the course of fulfilling the stages of the *cursus honorum* and having attained the age of 43, a Roman could seek election to the highest senatorial office in Rome, that of consul. Elected to a one-year term, a consul, together with his partner consul, entered into what might be called a dual presidency. Both of them had to agree for any initiative to become law. Either of them could veto the actions of any lower office holders. Thus they held the highest executive and judicial power in the land. Furthermore, they were the commanders of the army, with each of them having two legions under his command. This access to military power, when used unconstitutionally by strong consuls, eventually proved disastrous and hastened the unraveling of the republican form of government. In public, consuls were attended by 12 lictors.

Before speaking of the dissolution of the republic, we need to remind ourselves how well it worked when constitutional procedures were followed. It's easy to forget that from its founding in 509 B.C. until the changeover to an imperial form of government ushered in by Caesar Augustus was a span of some 480 years. God, of course, controls the destiny of nations but, humanly speaking, a great deal of the Roman republic's long and successful run can be credited to enlightened leadership. The Roman mind had a genius for law and order, both at home and when dealing with the provinces. E. M. Blaiklock makes this observation:

> It is part of the wonder of Roman history that . . . Rome resolved the vast tensions of her class struggle by debate, wise compromise, and a legal inventiveness which laid the foundations for another tremendous contribution of Rome to human history, namely, Roman law. (*Zondervan Pictorial Encyclopedia of the Bible*, s.v. "Rome")

Wise compromise was most readily observable at home, particularly in the steadily increasing input into government operations that was granted to the plebeian populace as it grew in numbers and wealth. In general, the senate's loss was the people's gain.

But even in assimilating conquered people, Rome generally displayed wisdom and humane practices. They did not, like the Assyrians and Babylonians, for example, try to destroy defeated nations by dividing them up and deporting them to the four corners of the empire. As a comparison, in the business world a monopolist tries to destroy and eliminate the competition. A conglomerate approach uses a merger and acquisitions approach, resulting in a strong and successful company. That's how the Romans operated.

If conquered people accepted the presence of an occupational army, paid their taxes, and generally lived quietly, they were allowed to stay in their land, to retain much of their local government, to keep their national religion, and to follow their traditional social customs. Things such as voting privileges, being required or permitted to serve in the army, and being allowed to mint money were open for negotiation between Rome and the occupied territory.

Rome's treatment of the provinces tended to remain pretty constant throughout the republican era. It was at home, however, that disconcerting changes led to the demise of the republic.

Constant warfare took its toll on the rank-and-file citizens who were expected to serve in the military for long periods of time in distant places. Often the farms they left behind were in shambles when they returned. Even worse was coming home to find their land taken over by aristocratic entrepreneurs. Tribute flowing into the capital from the provinces enabled well-placed individuals to accumulate tremendous wealth. Often they used their money to buy out small landholders and then combined these holdings into large tracts. They farmed these by employing the slaves that were readily available from among conquered nations.

The growing imbalance between the landed aristocracy and the dispossessed lower classes led to ever louder demands for constitutional changes to level the playing field. A telltale sign that the upper class had at this stage lost its capacity for wise compromise showed itself in their negative reaction to the sensible land reforms proposed by the Gracchus brothers. In separate incidents, both of them were killed by enraged senators and their henchmen—Tiberius in 133 B.C. and Gaius in 123 B.C. No punishment was ever meted out to the perpetrators. This act of violence may fairly be considered the start of a century-long downward spiral resulting in the undoing of the republic.

Driven from their land, many rural folks straggled into Rome. Unemployed and dispirited, crowded into the slums that grew up throughout the city and living on the public dole, they were an easy prey for any demagogue strongman promising them a better life, or at least the minimum perks of "bread and games."

Gaius Marius, elected seven times as consul, was one such strongman who recruited the poor and downtrodden for his army. With them he gained an impressive victory in north Africa. When he was also successful in putting down a revolt among some of Rome's allies, he felt he should have the command of a campaign to solidify Rome's eastern border. In this he was challenged by another strongman, his partner consul Lucius Sulla. Sulla threatened to march on Rome with his army and sack it if not given command of the expedition. The Roman senate was cowed into giving Sulla the command. The popular assembly, however, declared Marius the legitimate general to lead the expedition. Civil war followed. Marius was exiled to Africa but reassembled his army and marched on Rome. Clearly, things were no longer running along constitutional lines.

In 60 B.C. Julius Caesar, a strongman in his own right, made an alliance with two other powerful leaders to form what has come to be called the First Triumvirate. His collaborators in this power grab at the expense of the senate were the fabulously rich businessman

Marcus Crassus and the military hero Pompey the Great. Crassus was killed fighting the Parthians on the eastern border of the empire. Predictably, there soon was a falling out between Julius Caesar, who was a friend of Marius, whom the people supported, and Pompey, who sided with Sulla and the senate.

Caesar wasted little time in challenging his senatorial opponents. Thanks to a brilliant military campaign in Gaul (modern France), Caesar enjoyed immense prestige with the Roman populace. He also had the unswerving loyalty of his veteran army, which he declined to dismiss, as was constitutionally required of him. The outlying northern border of Italy proper was the Rubicon River. Crossing the Rubicon with army intact would be considered an attack on Rome and an act of treason.

Caesar crossed the Rubicon and in so doing issued a clear challenge to Pompey and the senate. Civil war ensued, with the outcome decided in 48 B.C. in the Battle of Pharsalus, where Pompey and his senatorial troops were routed. The defeated Pompey fled to Egypt, only to be assassinated by forces currying the favor of Caesar.

That left only the ambitious Caesar standing. Upon his return to Rome, he packed the senate with people loyal to himself, expanding that body to nine hundred members. Not surprisingly, this enlarged senate acceded to his proposal that he be granted "extraordinary powers." In effect, he was taking over all the functions ordinarily carried out by the various magistrates. Such an arrangement was not entirely new. It had been granted before to Sulla, but only for a limited time. What was new here was that Caesar had himself declared "dictator for life."

That was too much for many of the disempowered senators. A conspiracy of some 60 senators, led by Brutus and Cassius, brazenly stabbed the dictator to death in the senate chamber on the Ides of March, 44 B.C.

Subsequently, a Second Triumvirate arose, this one constitutionally formed to fill the void created by Caesar's death. It consisted of the consul Marc Antony, who was Caesar's second cousin; the successful general Marcus Lepidus, who had served as cavalry commander under Caesar; and Octavian, the youthful grand-nephew and adopted heir of Julius Caesar. This arrangement served for two five-year terms (43–33 B.C.), but eventually it came to a bad end, in many ways similar to that of the First Triumvirate.

It was predictable that a high priority on the Second Triumvirate's agenda would be punishing those involved in Caesar's assassination. And it was. Lists were drawn up, arbitrarily marking suspected conspirators for execution. No one was safe. No one trusted anyone—and with good reason. It was a dreadful time to be living in Rome! Things were not much better away from Rome. In the outlying areas as well, Roman fought against Roman. The arch-conspirators, Brutus and Cassius, were roundly defeated by Triumvirate forces in the Battle of Philippi (42 B.C.).

Because of his excessive personal ambitions, Lepidus was forced out of the Triumvirate. And because of Marc Antony's dallying with the Egyptian queen Cleopatra, they were suspected in Rome of contemplating the establishment of their own eastern empire. The inevitable clash took place in 31 B.C. in the sea battle of Actium, off the west coast of Greece. Octavian won; Antony and Cleopatra committed suicide. As at the conclusion of the First Triumvirate, when Julius Caesar was the only one left standing, so also here. Octavian alone was left. In all this, however, the Roman Republic was the greatest casualty.

The Roman Empire

In 29 B.C. the victorious Octavian returned home from the east to a war-weary country that wanted nothing more than peace. After all, there had been more than a century of strife and civil unrest, dating back to the unsuccessful attempt at land reform by the Gracchus brothers. Rome was ready to trade in its republican government for an autocracy that could keep the peace.

Under these circumstances the third stage of Roman history was ushered in. It is a period historians have come to call the Roman Empire. That is perhaps an unfortunate choice, since the term allows two meanings.

If one thinks of an empire in the geographical sense, namely, a dominant power drawing together a large number of dependencies under its control, then one would have to conclude that Rome had become an empire long before Octavian's time. Since 509 B.C. it had gradually expanded its territory to include much of Europe, north Africa, the Balkans, and the Middle East.

But the term *empire* can also refer to the Roman people allowing its republican privileges to reside in the person of an emperor. Octavian worked hard at creating and polishing his image as a loyal citizen and faithful servant of the state. When he returned home victorious after the Battle of Actium, even though urged by many to assume the role of dictator, Octavian dutifully surrendered all the extraordinary powers that had been granted to him in the previous time of crisis. He formally laid them aside—only to receive them all back constitutionally from a country that dreaded the thought of multiple leaders and more civil war.

On January 16, 27 B.C., the senate bestowed on Octavian the honorific title of "Augustus" (which means "illustrious one" or "venerable one"). In itself the title did not convey any constitutional power. Rather, it reflected the adulation and gratitude of an appreciative public.

The senate willingly agreed to have Octavian, or Augustus, hold the highest senatorial office of consul and to act in their stead. The general assembly also voted to give him the power of a *tribune*, the highest office representing the plebeian class. They also made him *pontifex maximus* (high priest). As such he could introduce measures to guide public ethics and morals and even to foster attempts at reviving the old traditional state religion.

The old republican forms remained, but they were hollow forms. Augustus nominated the candidates to be voted on by the senate for the various public offices. The general assembly still had a tribune chairing their meetings, but Augustus was given "tribunician powers" that allowed him to submit bills for the assembly to pass and gave him veto power. The fiction of shared power was carefully cultivated in all areas except one. Augustus was the *imperator*, the supreme military commander. There would be no victorious generals keeping their armies intact and then coming home to challenge the leadership and foment civil war.

The Roman Occupation of Palestine: A Sketch of Roman History

Caesar Augustus' rule as emperor lasted 41 years (27 B.C.–A.D. 14). It ushered in a long line of emperors after him. It was also the beginning of the *Pax Romana*, the remarkable "Roman peace" that for two centuries served so well not only for the Roman people but also and especially for the spread of the gospel and the establishment of the Christian church.

Subjugation and Occupation of Palestine

In those days Caesar Augustus issued a decree that a census should be taken of the entire Roman world. (Luke 2:1)

The Roman census of which Luke speaks extended over the "entire Roman world," which obviously included the Jews living in Judea. But how had they come under Roman control?

In reality, since the glory days of David and Solomon, the Jewish nation had experienced very little independence. The Assyrians carried off the Northern Kingdom in 722 B.C. Eventually the kingdom of Judah suffered the same fate, being carried off by the Babylonians in 586 B.C. After a 70-year captivity, Cyrus, the Persian conqueror of the Babylonians, allowed the Jews to return to their homeland, although relatively few accepted his offer.

Judea's client relationship with Persia came to an abrupt end when the Macedonian Alexander the Great overran the whole eastern Mediterranean region in the decade of 333–323 B.C. After Alexander's untimely death, his conquered territories fell to three of his generals. Antigonus received the home base of Macedonia; Seleucus took the region of Syria (which included Judea); and Ptolemy became the ruler of Egypt.

When the Seleucid rulers tried to force Greek customs on the Jews and Samaritans, they encountered fierce resistance from the Jewish nation. The nation revolted under the leadership of the Maccabees and for a short while gained their independence. But quarrels in the family over succession to the high priesthood eventually compromised that independence. Both sides sought help from the Romans. That "help" soon came in the person of the Roman general Pompey the Great. The camel had his nose in the tent, so to speak.

In 66 B.C. the Roman senate granted Pompey a three-year commission to serve in the eastern Mediterranean theater. His initial assignment was to clear out the Cilician pirates who had become a menace to the grain shipments from Egypt. With his usual efficiency, Pompey cured the pirate problem in three months. For the rest of the three years, he busied himself with shoring up the weak eastern border of the Roman Empire. Rome's concern was the possible westward expansion by the Seleucid rulers in Syria.

In 64 B.C. Pompey invaded Syria and Judea and captured Jerusalem. Judea was annexed to Syria and formally came under Roman rule in that same year when Syria was added to the growing list of Roman provinces. As such, Judea was subject to the census order issued by Caesar Augustus.

Roman Provinces

In the early days of the Roman Republic, the Latin word *provincia* (province) served to identify a magistrate's area of responsibility. For example, a quaestor's "province" would be fiscal affairs, an aedile's province would be the maintenance of temples and public buildings, etc. This terminology worked well enough while Roman territory was limited to Italy.

Things changed, however, when Rome expanded. Then, the term *province* came to refer to the place where the magistrate's duties were to be carried out.

A much-used expansion device, leading to the formation of new provinces, was Rome's standing offer to support a weaker party involved in a dispute with a stronger neighbor. Rome would help the weaker party defeat the troublesome neighbor, but it would then stay not only in the conquered enemy's territory but also leave a security force in the ally's territory. In the end, both came under Roman control.

After the occupation of a new territory, Rome would work out a carefully devised set of regulations with them, much like a constitution. This was worked out by the conquering general and a committee of ten men from the Roman senate. Major items were the payment of war reparations and setting the rate of ongoing taxes. Other items included setting up a court system, dividing the territory into workable administrative units, and determining how much of the local government could be utilized to administer the new system. Inclusion of the local leadership was an important aspect of Rome's dealing with provinces—and one that for a long time they handled very well.

During the time of the Republic, the provinces were all "senatorial." The senate chose one of its own, usually a former consul or praetor, to serve as governor of the province for one year. With the advent of the emperor, the procedure changed significantly. Some provinces came to be "imperial" provinces and were virtually the property of the emperor. Whereas tribute and taxes from the senatorial provinces flowed into the public treasury, the income from imperial provinces was basically at the emperor's disposal.

To administer one of his imperial provinces, the emperor would appoint as governor a legate who was usually not from the senate. This man might have officials ranked under him as *procurators* and *prefects*. Pontius Pilate was one such procurator, serving under the legate of the imperial province of Syria. The term of office for imperial appointments was indefinite. Many served for only a year. Pontius Pilate served for ten years.

By the end of the second half of the Roman Republic (241–29 B.C.), during which time the senate was annexing non-Italian territories, there were 17 provinces—all senatorial. During the first half of the Roman Empire, some 30 added provinces were a mix of senatorial and imperial. When Emperor Diocletian in the A.D. 290s reorganized the empire to allow closer supervision of subject dependencies, he ended up with almost one hundred provinces.

Provincial Administration

PROCONSULS

They [Paul, Barnabas, and John Mark] traveled through the whole island [Cyprus] until they came to Paphos. There they met a Jewish sorcerer and false prophet named Bar-Jesus, who was an attendant of

> *the proconsul, Sergius Paulus. The proconsul, an intelligent man, sent for Barnabas and Saul because he wanted to hear the word of God.* (Acts 13:6,7)

Although recording history was not the New Testament writers' main objective, the records they have left us are historically accurate. Because for many years nothing was known about any provincial administrator named Sergius Paulus, the accuracy of Luke's account in Acts chapter 13 was questioned. But that former gap in history has been filled.

> In 1877, an inscription was found near Paphos, bearing Sergius Paulus' name and title of proconsul. Ten years later, his name was also found on a memorial stone in Rome. The stone records that in A.D. 47 he was appointed as one of the keepers of the banks and channel of the river Tiber. He held this office when he retuned to Rome after his three years as governor of Cyprus. (www.facingthechallenge.org/paulus.php, accessed October 2010)

Luke is accurate in using the proper terms to identify the numerous provincial officials who turn up in his account. Calling Sergius Paulus the proconsul of Cyprus is a case in point, as a sketch of Rome's treatment of the island indicates.

Cyprus was too rich a source of copper for Rome not to set its eyes on this prize. In 58 B.C. Rome claimed it as one of its possessions. Administratively, Rome made Cyprus a part of the province of Cilicia. Under this arrangement Cilicia had a proconsul and Cyprus was ruled by a governor who ranked below the Cilician proconsul. This subservient arrangement for Cyprus is documented by the fact that one of its governors was none other than Cicero, the famous orator and literary figure. He has left a record of his one-year stint as governor.

At the time of Luke's writing, however, things had changed. When in 27 B.C. the republic changed into an empire, the emperor reorganized many of his dependencies and client holdings. In the course of the shuffle, Cyprus became a separate province. At first it was an imperial province, under the emperor's supervision, but it eventually became a senatorial province and thus was administered by senate-appointed proconsuls. Luke correctly describes the provincial administration that was in place when Paul and Barnabas were there:

> So Paul stayed [in Corinth] for a year and a half, teaching them the word of God.
>
> While Gallio was proconsul of Achaia, the Jews made a united attack on Paul and brought him into court. (Acts 18:11,12)

Corinth was the capital of the senatorial province of Achaia (Greece), so Luke is again using proper terminology when he describes the office of Gallio, the Roman administrator in charge, as being that of a proconsul. Among his many responsibilities, a proconsul was also the highest judge in his territory. More will be said later regarding Gallio's handling of the religious complaint here lodged against Paul by the local Jews.

Procurators

In addition to proconsuls, the New Testament writers refer also to another, somewhat lower, level of provincial officers. The Romans had a name for them, calling them *procurators*. In the gospels and Acts, they are referred to with the generic Greek term *hegemon* (leader), which the translators regularly render as "governor."

In the Roman Empire, the emperor usually selected middle-class citizens (knights or freedmen) for these supportive roles. The areas of service tended to fall into three main categories. Some procurators were sent out to help with tax collection. In fact, sometimes they were sent out specifically to keep an eye on rapacious and unscrupulous superiors. A second service category was helping with law enforcement and dealing with legal matters and serving in the court system. Of special interest to us here is the third category, of which R. C. Stone says:

> Some procurators governed minor provinces, such as Thrace and Judea. Here they were not restricted to financial matters, but had the power of life and death as any other governor. Most often they were semi dependent on the governors of larger provinces. (*Zondervan Pictorial Encyclopedia of the Bible*, s.v. "procurator")

> *Early in the morning, all the chief priests and the elders of the people came to the decision to put Jesus to death. They bound him, led him away and handed him over to Pilate, the governor.* (Matthew 27:1,2)

What is known about Pilate comes mostly from the gospels and the account of the Jewish historian Josephus. Both sources agree that he was callous and cruel, tactless and tyrannical, and at times weak and vacillating. He was the fifth procurator to serve in the "minor province" of Judea. Appointed by Tiberius in A.D. 26, he served for ten years, always answerable to Vitellius, the administrator of the much larger province of Syria. After Pilate's senseless massacre of many Samaritans, there was such an outcry that his superior Vitellius was forced to take action. He deposed him from office and sent him back to Rome to face charges before the emperor. Unsupported but frequently repeated accounts have him committing suicide.

In the course of describing Paul's dealing with the Roman legal system, Luke introduces us to a second Judean procurator, or governor. Luke does this by quoting a letter to the governor.

> *He [the commander] wrote a letter as follows:*
> *Claudius Lysias,*
> *To His Excellency, Governor Felix:*
> *Greetings.* (Acts 23:25,26)

Letters in New Testament times regularly took a standard form. First, the author introduced himself. Then, he named the person to whom the letter was addressed. Third, he added a word of greeting. All three elements clearly appear in the commander's letter to Felix.

How Luke obtained the text of the letter is unknown, but the letter does us the service of revealing the name of the commander who rescued Paul from the lynch mob in Jerusalem. It's a certain Claudius Lysias. And he is writing to his superior, Governor Felix. In Acts, Luke gives considerable information on how things worked in Paul's dealing with the provincial legal system that was administered by Felix. Before turning to that, however, it may be helpful to introduce a third procurator/governor mentioned by name in the New Testament Scriptures:

When two years had passed, Felix was succeeded by Porcius Festus, but because Felix wanted to grant a favor to the Jews, he left Paul in prison. (Acts 24:27)

Porcius Festus' two-year administration (A.D. 59–61) followed the seven-year rule of his predecessor, Felix. Luke says little about Festus because almost immediately upon the new governor's arrival, Paul opted out of his court by appealing to Caesar in Rome.

COMMANDERS

As Paul stopped at various cities on the return portion of his third missionary journey, there were repeated prophetic warnings that trouble awaited him in Jerusalem. Those prophecies came true when Paul was incorrectly assumed to have defiled the temple by bringing Gentiles into it. A Jewish mob formed and would have killed Paul had it not been for the intervention of the commander whom we now know from his letter as Claudius Lysias. While Paul was in the custody of this Roman commander, a Jewish plot against Paul's life was detected and foiled. Luke gives us a look at the circumstances:

When the son of Paul's sister heard of this plot, he went into the barracks and told Paul.

Then Paul called one of the centurions and said, "Take this young man to the commander; he has something to tell him." So he took him to the commander. (Acts 23:16-18)

One wishes Luke had said a bit more about the intriguing detail that, although Paul hailed from the city of Tarsus in Cilicia, he had relatives living in Jerusalem. They obviously were not hostile to Christianity, since they took measures to protect Paul and likely endangered themselves by leaking sensitive information to the Roman provincial government. Unfortunately, we have to settle for silence regarding any further family details about the young man other than that he was Paul's nephew and was kindly disposed toward him.

We can say a bit more, however, regarding the distinctly military setting in which all this took place. Paul was being held in the "barracks," the place where the soldiers stayed. Usually that was close to the *praetorium*, the headquarters where the commander resided and where official business was done, particularly court cases and legal matters.

Two levels of military rank are evident in this incident. The rank of centurion is fairly straightforward; he's the leader of a hundred men. The word translated as "commander," however, is being handled more interpretively. Luke is here using the Greek word *chiliarch*. Literally it means the officer over a *thousand* men. The Roman military, however, did not have units with that number, so the translators are substituting a workable equivalent when they use the generic term *commander*.

To get an idea of the actual number of troops involved in the various divisions of the Roman army, we have to look at the makeup of a Roman legion. Understandably, the size and the tactics of a legion evolved considerably over Rome's long career, incorporating the changes from monarchy to republic to empire.

Originally, since the time of Greek and Macedonian supremacy in the east, the phalanx system was predominant. Basically, it was a rectangular formation of spearmen, at least three rows deep—sometimes as deep as five or six rows. The back rows had spears with longer shafts, extending their spear points out about the same distance as the spears held by the front rows. As it bore down on the enemy, the phalanx projected a fearsome wall of spear points, something like the quills of a giant porcupine. Unfortunately, the system also had some weaknesses. It could operate effectively only on fairly level ground, and it tended to be vulnerable to side attacks and ambush from the rear.

The Roman legion of New Testament times was greatly improved by the addition of men skilled in javelin throwing. These men in the front row(s) were each equipped with two short throwing spears, or javelins. Hence the first assault on the enemy was a shower of spears descending on them. After delivering their two volleys of javelins, these spearmen would drop back in the ranks to allow the infantry, the mainline "legionnaires," to come into the fray. Heavily armed and armored, these troops charged the enemy who were still trying to get reorganized after the hail of javelins. Roman field generals were very careful to intermingle seasoned troops with inexperienced soldiers in the middle rows. If things got too intense, the middle rows could give way to the anchor men of the back row(s), the battle-hardened veterans of previous campaigns.

Because each man had to provide his own equipment, the offensive weapons of the legionnaire varied somewhat from one age to another, but the main three always were a sturdy thrusting spear, a large slashing sword, and a short dagger. Defensive armor consisted of a helmet, body armor of various designs, a belt and sheath for holding a dagger, greaves (shin guards) on the legs, and good sturdy boots. All this was covered by a large rectangular shield, often curved to provide some side protection as well as frontal protection.

In the closing chapter of his letter to the Ephesians, the apostle Paul mentions virtually all of these items. He urges Christians to defend themselves against the attacks of the evil one by using the Word as belt and breastplate (6:14), boots and shield (6:15,16), helmet and sword (6:17). This would have been meaningful imagery, particularly for retired military personnel, of which there were many in the Mediterranean world during New Testament times. Philippi, for example, was a Roman colony often referred to as "Little Rome" because of the many retired solders who had been given land grants there.

It has already been mentioned that a major improvement to the Roman legion's tactical capabilities was the addition of spear-throwing soldiers. Another major improvement was developing a useful corps of auxiliary troops to protect the flanks and rear of the legion. These forces consisted in part of cavalry—knights from the middle class often working their way toward acceptance into the patrician class. There were also light-armed infantry who were much more mobile than the heavy-armed troops. These foot soldiers wore lighter armor and used smaller shields. Some brought specialty skills, such as slingers or archers. Often these were non-Romans from the provinces who were looking to be given citizenship and a retirement package when they were mustered out after 25 years of service.

Little is known of the initial stages of the Roman military machine. Tradition dates it back to Rome's founder, Romulus, who reportedly had three thousand foot soldiers and three hundred auxiliary troops. Obviously the numbers increased as the empire grew, but the proportion of legionnaires to auxiliary troops remained fairly constant. Originally only Roman citizens from the Italian regions in the "boot" of Italy were eligible for military service. They owed military service in lieu of paying taxes and were subject to call whenever the need for military action arose in the provinces. Eventually subjects from the provinces became integrated into the empire and loyal enough to be trusted not to turn against Rome in the heat of battle. That job opportunity drew many volunteers from the provinces, and Rome soon came to depend on them as a standing mercenary army.

How large was this army in New Testament times? One can get an indication by looking at the situation in the days of Caesar Augustus. He suffered a disastrous setback at the hands of Arminius (a.k.a. Herman the German). In the year A.D. 9, this crafty and unreliable tribal leader lured the Roman general Varus into the inhospitable terrain of the Teutoburg Forest, where he annihilated three Roman legions. Roman records indicate that this defeat reduced the Roman army to 25 legions.

But how many men would that have left? One obviously would have to know the number of men in a legion, and that unfortunately is something of a moving target. W. White ventures an estimate when he says, "By the end of the first century A.D., the legion contained about 6,000 men when up to full strength. More often than not, they were under this figure by as much as thirty-three percent" (*Zondervan Pictorial Encyclopedia of the Bible*, s.v. "legion"). So the standing army of 25 legions at Christ's time, deployed around the empire at various borders, might have numbered somewhere between 100,000 and 150,000 legionnaires, plus the auxiliary troops and the commanding officers.

W. White also comments on the standard divisions within the legion, together with their commanding officers: "The legion was subdivided into ten cohorts and these were divided into six centuries or 'hundreds' each. The officer in charge of this last division was the *centurion*, 'leader of one hundred' mentioned often in the NT. . . . Over the whole legion there was the *tribuni militum*, 'military tribune,' with his subordinate the *legatus*, 'lieutenant–general' " (*Zondervan Pictorial Encyclopedia of the Bible*, s.v. "legion").

The role centurions played in the Roman army, and also to a considerable degree in numerous New Testament events, can be reserved for the next section. But before leaving the current discussion of commanders, we can tie up a loose end. Recall that when Luke referred to Claudius Lysias rescuing Paul, he used the term *chiliarch* (ruler of a thousand). It was noted at the time that there was no Roman army position corresponding exactly to such an office. Hence, the generic translation of "commander" was favored by the translators. Note that in preparation for moving Paul to Caesarea, this "commander" gave orders to two centurions to get the needed security forces together. He could possibly have been the "military tribune" that W. White speaks of or, more likely, his lieutenant *(legatus)*.

CENTURIONS

A centurion was a junior officer in charge of a *century*, that is, one hundred men. With six centuries per cohort and ten cohorts per legion, there would have been some 60 centurions in each legion of the Roman army. Predictably, some of them turn up in the scriptural record.

Most of the centurions referred to in the New Testament are nameless, faceless people just doing their jobs. A centurion was in charge of Christ's crucifixion (Matthew 27:54). A centurion was on the scene at the near scourging of Paul in Jerusalem (Acts 22:25). Two centurions headed up the detail of moving the prisoner Paul from Jerusalem to Caesarea (Acts 23:23). None of them receives any negative comment. Four, in fact, are reported favorably. Matthew, Mark, and Luke all cite the confession made by the centurion at Golgotha:

> *When the centurion, who stood there in front of Jesus, heard his cry and saw how he died, he said, "Surely this man was the Son of God!"* (Mark 15:39)

Also nameless but highly commended is the centurion of Capernaum:

> *When Jesus had entered Capernaum, a centurion came to him, asking for help. "Lord," he said, "my servant lies at home paralyzed and in terrible suffering."*
>
> *Jesus said to him, "I will go and heal him."*

> *The centurion replied, "Lord, I do not deserve to have you come under my roof. But just say the word, and my servant will be healed. For I myself am a man under authority, with soldiers under me. I tell this one, 'Go,' and he goes; and that one, 'Come,' and he comes. I say to my servant, 'Do this,' and he does it."*
>
> *When Jesus heard this, he was astonished and said to those following him, "I tell you the truth, I have not found anyone in Israel with such great faith."* (Matthew 8:5-10)

Because Jesus contrasts this centurion's faith with that of the Israelites, the centurion undoubtedly was a Gentile who had converted to Judaism. He would appear to have been fairly wealthy, for Luke in his account adds the people's plea, "This man deserves to have you do this, because he loves our nation and has built our synagogue" (Luke 7:4b,5).

Note how the centurion describes his status as a junior officer. The power he has from above enables him to deal authoritatively with those below. In this he sees a corollary to Jesus' situation. With the power Jesus as true God has from above, he can easily, even without being on location, deal with the problem of sickness in a beloved servant. The centurion was not disappointed.

In the eyes of his Jewish neighbors, this centurion was a model citizen, but infinitely more important than kudos from the local people is Jesus' commendation, "I have not found anyone in Israel with such great faith" (Matthew 8:10). Well might we all pray, "Lord, give us such faith."

CORNELIUS

> *At Caesarea there was a man named Cornelius, a centurion in what was known as the Italian Regiment. He and all his family were devout and God-fearing; he gave generously to those in need and prayed to God regularly.* (Acts 10:1,2)

The Roman army made good use of standards, banners, ensigns, etc. Each legion had a silver or bronze eagle as its distinctive feature. The eagle was mounted on a pole sharpened at its base. Thus it could be stuck in the ground to indicate to the troops where they were to assemble. Or it could be carried by a specially designated soldier honored with the title of "eagle bearer." His eagle would lead the way during a march or serve as a rallying point in battle. Or in dangerous situations the eagle's staff could even be turned around and used by the eagle bearer as a spear.

The smaller divisions, the cohorts (or regiments), also had identifying signs. Their sign often was a pole with a crossbar to which was attached a square piece of colored fabric with something distinctive embroidered into the panel. Many started out with a number, but as numbers became duplicated by other units, something more was needed. Often the nationality of the soldiers in the unit was featured. Sometimes a ferocious animal was pictured. The wild boar was a favorite. With his Latin name, it is not surprising that Cornelius belonged to the Italian Regiment.

What is a bit unusual is the reference to "all his family." Some have theorized that he was an enlisted man from the area of Caesarea with family and relatives still around. That seems unlikely with his Latin name, unless he took the name later to reflect his allegiance to Rome. Perhaps a more plausible explanation is that "family" is used to refer to the extended family that included household servants and friends (see Acts 10:24,27).

> *One day at about three in the afternoon [Cornelius] had a vision. He distinctly saw an angel of God, who came to him and said, "Cornelius . . . send men to Joppa to bring back a man named Simon who is called Peter."* (Acts 10:3,5)

Cornelius gets almost as good a review as did the centurion in Capernaum. He is described as devout, God-fearing, generous, and diligent in prayer. But by God's grace he was chosen for another distinction, to be bestowed on him through a visit from Peter.

Meanwhile in Joppa, Peter in a trance saw a vision of a great sheet let down from heaven full of all sorts of animals, unclean under Jewish law, of which Peter declined to take and eat. The Lord curtly rebuked him with the words, "Do not call anything impure that God has made clean" (Acts 10:15). This was a picture of God opening the door for Gentiles to be welcomed into the Christian church as equal partners with the Jews. That, however, became clear to Peter only after he dutifully accompanied the messengers and entered Cornelius' house. Luke reports:

> *Then Peter began to speak: "I now realize how true it is that God does not show favoritism but accepts men from every nation who fear him and do what is right. You know the message God sent to the people of Israel, telling the good news of peace through Jesus Christ, who is Lord of all."*
>
> *While Peter was still speaking these words, the Holy Spirit came on all who heard the message. The circumcised believers who had come with Peter were astonished that the gift of the Holy Spirit had been poured out even on the Gentiles. For they heard them speaking in tongues and praising God.*
>
> *Then Peter said, "Can anyone keep these people from being baptized with water? They have received the Holy Spirit just as we have." So he ordered that they be baptized in the name of Jesus Christ.* (Acts 10:34-36,44-48)

When Peter preached "the good news of peace through Jesus Christ, who is Lord of all," Cornelius and his household believed the message. But faith in the heart is invisible. That is why the Holy Spirit gave clear evidence of his saving work by letting Peter's listeners speak in tongues. How necessary this tangible proof was is evident from the amazement on the part of Peter's Jewish companions. Astonished, they cried out, "So then, God has granted even the Gentiles repentance unto life" (Acts 11:18).

It is worth noting that Scripture records three instances in which the Holy Sprit gave clear testimony that he was ushering in a new stage in the history of the Christian church. The first was on Pentecost in Jerusalem, the birthday of the New Testament Christian church. There he dealt with a largely Jewish congregation. The second instance was in response to Philip's work in Samaria (Acts 8:14-17), where the Holy Spirit clearly approved the acceptance into the Christian church of half-Jewish Samaritans. And here in Caesarea we see the acceptance of full Gentiles. The Lord in his grace chose Cornelius, a rough Roman centurion, to be his poster boy, certifying full acceptance of Gentiles into the Christian church. The arrival of the Magi is often referred to as "the Gentiles' Christmas." In a real sense, this outpouring of the Spirit in the home of Cornelius could well be called "the Gentiles' Pentecost."

JULIUS

When it was decided that we would sail for Italy, Paul and some other prisoners were handed over to a centurion named Julius, who belonged to the Imperial Regiment. We boarded a ship from Adramyttium about to sail for ports along the coast of the province of Asia, and we put out to sea. Aristarchus, a Macedonian from Thessalonica, was with us. (Acts 27:1,2)

Because Paul could not get his case resolved in the provincial court system, he appealed to Caesar. But that meant making a sea journey from Caesarea to Rome. In connection with that transfer, Paul the prisoner came under the watchful eye of a Roman centurion named Julius. Paul was not the only prisoner being transferred, and Julius was not alone in guarding them, as becomes evident when Luke later speaks of "soldiers" being aboard (Acts 27:31,32,42). They undoubtedly were members of the Imperial Cohort, as Julius was.

When reading Acts, it is important to keep an eye out for the "we" passages. They indicate when Luke is accompanying the apostle Paul, which is much of the time. Luke is on board the ship along with Paul, together with Aristarchus, another of Paul's coworkers.

No doubt the ship was sailing back to its home port of Adramyttium on the Asia Minor coast, so it would not be going all the way to Rome. A change would have to be made en route.

The next day we landed at Sidon; and Julius, in kindness to Paul, allowed him to go to his friends so they might provide for his needs. From there we put out to sea again and passed to the lee of Cyprus because the winds were against us. (Acts 27:3,4)

In the course of making stops along the way, the ship put in at Sidon, where Julius "in kindness to Paul" allowed him to check in with friends. As indicated previously, ocean travel was no luxury cruise. Passengers were basically hitchhikers on freighters, camping out on the open deck. As a prisoner, Paul had no opportunity to provide for the necessities of life, so he looked to his friends in Sidon to supply his basic needs. Luke acknowledges that this was a special kindness on Julius' part.

Paul must have been a remarkably dynamic person, to judge from the immediate bond that developed between him and Julius. Or had Julius gotten to know him already during Paul's two-year imprisonment in Caesarea? At any rate, Julius was not only concerned about his prisoner's personal needs, but as we shall see, at times he even took advice from him. To onlookers, this must certainly have been an odd couple.

> *When we had sailed across the open sea off the coast of Cilicia and Pamphylia, we landed at Myra in Lycia. There the centurion found an Alexandrian ship sailing for Italy and put us on board.* (Acts 27:5,6)

Taking leave of the Palestinian and Phoenician coast, the ship headed out on the high seas and arrived at the Asia Minor coast town of Myra. From there it would port-hop northward toward its home base of Adramyttium. Hence, it was the end of the line for passengers heading to Rome. Julius had to find another ship heading west. There were no reservations. Travelers took their chances.

> *We made slow headway for many days and had difficulty. . . . The wind did not allow us to hold our course. . . . We moved along the coast with difficulty. . . . Much time had been lost, and sailing had already become dangerous because by now it was after the Fast.* (Acts 27:7-9)

The litany of problems in Luke's account leaves no doubt that the ship, buffeted by strong westerly headwinds, was in trouble.

> *So Paul warned them, "Men, I can see that our voyage is going to be disastrous and bring great loss to ship and cargo, and to our own lives also." But the centurion, instead of listening to what Paul said, followed the advice of the pilot and of the owner of the ship.* (Acts 27:9-11)

Something obviously had to be done, but one is surprised to find that Paul the prisoner had become a part of the planning committee. It is equally surprising that a centurion could make the decision to follow the advice of a pilot and shipowner, but that is what Luke reports.

> *After the men had gone a long time without food, Paul stood up before them and said: "Men, you should have taken my advice not to sail*

> *from Crete; then you would have spared yourselves this damage and loss. But now I urge you to keep up your courage, because not one of you will be lost; only the ship will be destroyed."* (Acts 27:21,22)

It is mildly amusing that after this bad decision by Julius and the crew, even great Paul could not resist the temptation to allow himself an "I-told-you-so." But he also had words of encouragement, based on the vision God had granted him the night before.

> *The ship struck a sandbar and ran aground. The bow stuck fast and would not move, and the stern was broken to pieces by the pounding of the surf.* (Acts 27:41)

After being storm-tossed for 14 days, land finally appeared. Not knowing that it was the island of Malta, they planned to make a run for it into a small bay, but even that went awry.

In Luke's last formal mention of Julius, we see the centurion in his finest hour. With the ship breaking up in the surf, counter to military prudence, Julius made a noble decision:

> *The soldiers planned to kill the prisoners to prevent any of them from swimming away and escaping. But the centurion wanted to spare Paul's life and kept them from carrying out their plan. He ordered those who could swim to jump overboard first and get to land. The rest were to get there on planks or on pieces of the ship. In this way everyone reached land in safety.* (Acts 27:42-44)

At first it must surely have seemed an unlikely combination, guard and prisoner teamed up together. But together they accomplished under God precisely what had been promised to Paul in his night vision: "Do not be afraid, Paul," the Lord had told him. "You must stand trial before Caesar; and God has graciously given you the lives of all who sail with you" (Acts 27:24).

The Roman Legal System

Paul had to "stand trial before Caesar" in Rome, but that was at the conclusion of a sequence of events that started much earlier at the provincial level. Let's return to the events that took place shortly after Paul's escape from the mob in Jerusalem and his being taken into custody by the Roman soldiers:

> *So the soldiers, carrying out their orders, took Paul with them during the night and brought him as far as Antipatris. The next day they let the cavalry go on with him, while they returned to the barracks.* (Acts 23:31,32)

Recall that when it was disclosed to the Roman commander Lysias that there was a Jewish plot against Paul, he sent him under heavy guard from Jerusalem to Caesarea, the provincial capital. Jerusalem always remained the religious capital of Judea, and as such it was a hotbed of nationalistic hopes and aspirations. That is why a strong military force needed to be quartered there at all times. This allowed Lysias to transfer Paul with an escort of two hundred soldiers, two hundred spearmen, and seventy cavalrymen.

Antipatris was a garrison city on the road to Caesarea, some 40 miles northwest of Jerusalem. After a rest stop at Antipatris, it would be an easy 20-mile leg for the cavalry to reach Caesarea.

The Judean coastline of the Mediterranean is singularly lacking in natural harbors. Hence, Herod had to build one from scratch. Twelve years in the making, Caesarea was a tribute to Herod's determination, engineering skill, and deep pockets. In water at some places 120 feet deep (20 fathoms), Herod built a breakwater 200 feet wide using huge limestone blocks, some as large as 50' x 10' x 9'. Herod displayed his pro-Roman bias by calling the city Caesarea and naming its harbor Port Augustus.

FELIX

> *When the cavalry arrived in Caesarea, they delivered the letter to the governor and handed Paul over to him. The governor read the letter and asked what province he was from. Learning that he was from Cilicia, he said, "I will hear your case when your accusers get here." Then he ordered that Paul be kept under guard in Herod's palace.* (Acts 23:33-35)

As the letter from commander Lysias informed us, the governor in Caesarea was Felix. After reading the letter, Felix inquired as to where Paul's citizenship was registered. As indicated previously, larger provinces occasionally had smaller provinces attached to them. In New Testament times, the eastern seaboard of the Mediterranean was basically the province of Syria. Judea was a minor province whose administrator, a procurator, was subordinate to the proconsul of Syria. A similar arrangement apparently existed at this time also with Cilicia. (Cilicia is on the extreme southeast corner of Asia Minor. It is the location of Tarsus, where Paul grew up.) Like Judea, it too was technically a part of Syria. Hence, it was within Felix's legal domain to try the case of a person from Cilicia.

Legally, everything appeared to be progressing in good order. Felix said he would not prejudge the case but would wait until both sides could make their presentations. Meanwhile, Paul was to be kept in Herod's praetorium, which the NIV translators render as "Herod's palace." Readers familiar with the KJV will remember the translation "Herod's judgment hall." Recall that a praetor held the second-highest office in the sequence of Roman political offices. His primary task was that of enforcing legal matters. When a Roman citizen was appointed to serve as a provincial governor (procurator), he also became responsible for handling legal matters. In effect, he was serving as a praetor. Hence, a praetorium could be both the place where a governor resided ("palace") or the place where he carried out his legal functions ("judgment hall"). In the present case, it was Herod's praetorium in the sense that he had built it. Herod had died some 50 years before Paul's arrival in Caesarea.

> Then Felix, who was well acquainted with the Way, adjourned the proceedings. "When Lysias the commander comes," he said, "I will decide your case." He ordered the centurion to keep Paul under guard but to give him some freedom and permit his friends to take care of his needs. (Acts 24:22,23)

The Romans were geniuses for organization. They were good at maintaining law and order—hence, the *Pax Romana*, Roman peace. In general, the peace and quiet that marked the empire was a tribute to good governance of the provinces. Two terms historians often use to characterize Roman rule are *fair* but *firm*. Roman expectations were reasonable, and they were consistently enforced.

As noted earlier, Scripture gives us a picture of four centurions, all of whom get very favorable reviews. Presumably the majority of governors were men of honesty and integrity as well. Unfortunately, the Roman governors described in Scripture get low grades. Pilate was not firm in opposing the murderous Jews. Felix was not fair in the trial he gave (or rather failed to give) Paul.

Luke tells us that five days after Paul's arrival in Caesarea, the Jerusalem Jews came to testify against him. Felix was well aware of the point of disagreement between the two parties, for he was acquainted with "the Way," which is simply an early term for Christianity. When he could have and should have given a verdict, he stalled with the hollow promise, "When Lysias the commander comes, I will decide your case." The dark side of his character that caused this delay soon becomes evident:

> *Several days later Felix came with his wife Drusilla, who was a Jewess. He sent for Paul and listened to him as he spoke about faith in Christ Jesus. As Paul discoursed on righteousness, self-control and the judgment to come, Felix was afraid and said, "That's enough for now! You may leave. When I find it convenient, I will send for you." At the same time he was hoping that Paul would offer him a bribe, so he sent for him frequently and talked with him.* (Acts 24:24-26)

Felix displays two negative traits here. When Paul preaches repentance to him, the governor hardens his heart and stalls once again. But the delaying tactic isn't simply a device to get himself out of an uncomfortable spot. His actions are also driven by the reprehensible wish to get a bribe from Paul. Things do not improve with the arrival of a new governor.

PORCIUS FESTUS

> *When two years had passed, Felix was succeeded by Porcius Festus, but because Felix wanted to grant a favor to the Jews, he left Paul in prison.* (Acts 24:27)

It would have been appropriate for Felix to close out his administration by taking care of the loose ends that needed attention. But shamefully, he did not do so. To do the Jews a favor, he left Paul lying in prison. And unfortunately, the new governor was inclined to continue this conciliatory policy toward the Jews, at Paul's expense.

> *Three days after arriving in the province, Festus went up from Caesarea to Jerusalem, where the chief priests and Jewish leaders appeared before him and presented the charges against Paul. They urgently requested Festus, as a favor to them, to have Paul transferred to Jerusalem, for they were preparing an ambush to kill him along the way.* (Acts 25:1-3)

Although Caesarea was the provincial capital of Judea and the site of the governor's official residence, Jerusalem always remained the religious capital. It would have been a bad mistake for the new governor not to check in with the Jewish leaders upon his arrival in the province. Three days after arriving, Festus paid his respects in Jerusalem. At once he found himself heavily lobbied by the same group that had previously plotted to kill Paul. Festus was firm enough in insisting that the accusers come to Caesarea and present their case there, which they did.

But when they arrived, he obstructed justice by putting the defendant, Paul, in a very compromised position:

> *When Paul appeared, the Jews who had come down from Jerusalem stood around him, bringing many serious charges against him, which they could not prove.*
>
> *Then Paul made his defense: "I have done nothing wrong against the law of the Jews or against the temple or against Caesar."*
>
> *Festus, wishing to do the Jews a favor, said to Paul, "Are you willing to go up to Jerusalem and stand trial before me there on these charges?"* (Acts 25:7-9)

Paul's Appeal to Caesar

As in Felix's case, Festus could have and should have given a verdict, but his conciliatory policy toward the Jews obstructed the justice Paul had a right to expect from the Roman legal system. In total frustration, Paul made his appeal to a higher court:

> *Paul answered: "I am now standing before Caesar's court, where I ought to be tried. I have not done any wrong to the Jews, as you*

> *yourself know very well. If, however, I am guilty of doing anything deserving death, I do not refuse to die. But if the charges brought against me by these Jews are not true, no one has the right to hand me over to them. I appeal to Caesar!"* (Acts 25:10,11)

In lodging an appeal, Paul was using a legal device that had been put into place only a relatively short time before. Under the Roman Republic, a judge's decision could not be challenged. It was only under Emperor Augustus and successive emperors that appeals came to be allowed.

With the various levels of appellate court that we're used to, it might seem like a gigantic leap for Paul's case to rise to the top level in one bound. Recall, however, that Judea was an imperial province, that is, one in which the emperor made administrative appointments, not the senate. *The Oxford Classical Dictionary* states, "[An appeal's] effect is that the controversy is brought before a higher magistrate, normally before the one who appointed the magistrate of the lower instance" (s.v. "appellatio"). Hence, Caesar's appointee was responsible directly to Caesar.

Festus may soon have come to regret his posturing to the Jews, because once the appeal was lodged, Festus was stuck with doing the required paperwork. Again *The Oxford Classical Dictionary* explains, "The magistrate whose decision was impugned... was then obliged to transmit all the documents of the case to the competent higher magistrate with a written report" (s.v. "appellatio"). This requirement proved to be a distinct embarrassment to the governor—so much so that he enlisted the help of the Herodian Agrippa, a minor king, when Agrippa came to pay his respects to the new governor. As Paul was brought in to testify before Agrippa, Festus acknowledged his dilemma:

> *"I found he had done nothing deserving of death, but because he made his appeal to the Emperor I decided to send him to Rome. But I have nothing definite to write to His Majesty about him. Therefore I have brought him before all of you, and especially before you, King Agrippa, so that as a result of this investigation I may have something to write. For I think it is unreasonable to send on a prisoner without specifying the charges against him."* (Acts 25:25-27)

The governor fudges the facts a bit, making it sound as though it was at his initiative that Paul was being sent to Rome. It was actually Paul's request as a Roman citizen, and Festus was obliged to honor it.

Roman Citizenship

As [the soldiers] stretched him out to flog him, Paul said to the centurion standing there, "Is it legal for you to flog a Roman citizen who hasn't even been found guilty?"

When the centurion heard this, he went to the commander and reported it. "What are you going to do?" he asked. "This man is a Roman citizen."

The commander went to Paul and asked, "Tell me, are you a Roman citizen?"

"Yes, I am," he answered.

Then the commander said, "I had to pay a big price for my citizenship."

"But I was born a citizen," Paul replied.

Those who were about to question him withdrew immediately. The commander himself was alarmed when he realized that he had put Paul, a Roman citizen, in chains. (Acts 22:25-29)

Again, we return to the series of events that took place shortly after Paul was taken into custody in Jerusalem. His exchange with the commander gives us an opportunity to talk about Roman citizenship.

The Romans were masters at governing defeated people and subject territories. As a general rule, they provided administrative and legal systems that were firm and fair. If at all workable, they allowed local institutions to continue functioning. They were also unusually generous in granting Roman citizenship to foreigners. There were at least five ways of obtaining citizenship. The passage cited above lists two of them.

The most highly regarded citizenship was that which came from being born Roman. Eventually the requirements changed, but for a long time both parents had to be Roman, otherwise the children would be considered foreigners.

A second method was by purchase. It wasn't cheap, as the Roman commander acknowledged to Paul, but it was possible. Many slaves and foreigners were highly qualified people capable of earning and accumulating money. And with the benefits citizenship brought, buying it was a good investment.

A third method was earning one's citizenship by military service. Those who signed up as legionnaires received immediate citizenship. The more lightly regarded auxiliary troops received citizenship upon being mustered out after 25 years of service.

The fourth and fifth methods are basically variations of the same thing. In the days of the Roman Republic, the senate could grant citizenship by legislation, and in the Roman Empire, the emperor could arbitrarily grant it on his own.

But what were the benefits of citizenship? The passage cited previously gives a number of examples. For one thing, it was illegal to put a Roman in chains publicly. To be sure, Paul in his epistles speaks of being "a prisoner in chains," but that was private detention, not public humiliation.

Also, it was illegal to beat a Roman citizen or to subject him to torture or physical injury. Even in the case of a capital crime, there were regulations as to how the criminal was to be executed. For example, a Roman citizen could not be crucified. Hence, tradition asserts that Peter and Paul were martyred on the same day, Peter by being crucified upside down and Paul by beheading.

A Roman citizen had the right to a fair trial, as Paul insinuates in his question to the soldiers in Jerusalem: "Is it legal for you to flog a Roman citizen who hasn't even been found guilty?" Festus acknowledged the same when he explained to King Agrippa, "I told [the Jews] that it is not the Roman custom to hand over any man before he has faced his accusers and has had an opportunity to defend himself against their charges" (Acts 25:16). And as Paul's case shows, a Roman citizen had the right to appeal if he felt the trial he had gotten wasn't just. There was, incidentally, a heavy fine for lodging a frivolous appeal.

Extrabiblical sources document other benefits. An important privilege was the right to enter into legally binding contracts. Often citizenship brought voting privileges. Occasionally there were exemptions from certain taxes or military service.

Roman Census

Just how did a person with Roman citizenship prove that he was a citizen? There is no indication that Paul was a "card carrying" citizen. It seems, in Paul's case at least, that citizenship was verbally claimed. The commander in Jerusalem ordered Paul, "Tell me, are you a Roman citizen?" Paul answered, "Yes, I am" (Acts 22:27). The commander considered Paul's word ample validation and accepted his claim.

But what was to keep a noncitizen from faking it? Some have stated that it was a capital crime, worthy of summary execution. An added deterrent was that such deceit could easily be exposed by checking the official records. That's where the census comes into play.

During the days of the Roman Republic, census taking in the Italian provinces in the boot of Italy was a rather regular occurrence. It determined who owed military service and who owed taxes. Wealth flowing in from the provinces eventually cancelled the need for the Italians to pay taxes. Recruits from the provinces constituted a standing army, so there was no need for compulsory military service. Consequently, census taking became infrequent in Italy but increased in the provinces.

It has been stated that the last days of the republic were dreadfully chaotic with political coups, assassinations, and civil war. A war-weary Rome wanted peace, and it received that from the peaceful emperors who ushered in the imperial age. Caesar Augustus (27 B.C.–A.D. 14) refrained from trying to extend the empire. Instead, he concentrated on solidifying his borders and restoring order within the empire. To do that he had to know what resources he had to work with.

> *In those days Caesar Augustus issued a decree that a census should be taken of the entire Roman world. (This was the first census that took*

place while Quirinius was governor of Syria.) And everyone went to his own town to register. (Luke 2:1-3)

The word translated "census" could also be rendered "enrollment." The information collected consisted mainly of two items: (a) family details and (b) property owned.

Some of the census papers record a suffocating amount of detail. E. M. Blaiklock cites an example from a census paper dated A.D. 48. It describes one member of the household as "about sixty-five years of age, of medium height, with honey colored complexion, having a long face and a scar on the right knee" (*Zondervan Pictorial Encyclopedia of the Bible*, s.v. "census"). With such detail officially recorded, surely the important matter of citizenship, if applicable, would also be included. The amount of property a person held determined the owner's tax liability.

In his long administration of 41 years, Caesar Augustus held three general censuses. The one that comes closest to the time of Jesus' birth is 7 B.C. Although it was a general census, it seems not to have been held at the same time in all the provinces of the empire. Blaiklock suggests that it "was held tardily in the turbulent Jewish province because of the covert resistance of Herod" (*Zondervan Pictorial Encyclopedia of the Bible*, s.v. "census").

Always careful with details, Luke tells us this was a "first census." At Acts 5:37 he refers to another, apparently later, census in Galilee. That one turned violent, likely because of the exorbitant taxes that Rome could levy after having determined by the census what property individuals had.

Roman Taxes

Wherever possible, Rome left in place the governing institutions of conquered people. The cost of continuing this self-rule, of course, was borne by the people just as before they were overrun by Rome. Unfortunately, with the arrival of the Romans, there came a whole new layer of tax obligation. That was the "tribute" Rome extracted from subject people. Tribute took the form of either direct or indirect tax.

> *As Jesus went on from [Capernaum], he saw a man named Matthew sitting at the tax collector's booth. "Follow me," he told him, and Matthew got up and followed him.* (Matthew 9:9)

For people living in the provinces, one of the less-appreciated benefits of the fine Roman road system was that it channeled traffic through fairly narrow corridors where it could be controlled with checkpoints and tollbooths. Capernaum was situated on the intersection of two major roads. Matthew was undoubtedly manning one of the tollbooths set up to levy tariffs on goods in transit. This was an indirect tax, but everyone knew it raised the cost of goods for the merchant, who in turn passed these costs on to the customer. The only one who benefited was Rome. Although collectors at tollbooths didn't take money directly from the pockets of the general public, they were much disliked for cooperating with the Romans.

> *Jesus entered Jericho and was passing through. A man was there by the name of Zacchaeus; he was a chief tax collector and was wealthy.*
>
> *But Zacchaeus stood up and said to the Lord, "Look, Lord! Here and now I give half of my possessions to the poor, and if I have cheated anybody out of anything, I will pay back four times the amount."* (Luke 19:1,2,8)

If collectors of indirect taxes such as road tolls were disliked, the agents of direct taxes on individuals were positively despised. These were the publicans, of whom Zacchaeus was not simply an ordinary worker, but a "chief tax collector."

From its census, Rome knew the relative wealth of all the people in a province. The percentage of this wealth that they demanded as annual tribute seems to have varied, but occasionally it ran as high as ten percent. Rome "farmed out" the dirty work of collecting taxes from individuals. There were companies that bid on contracts, giving them the privilege of collecting for Rome the assessed amount, plus a surcharge for themselves. The system reeked of graft and corruption. Repentant Zacchaeus, the little man who climbed a tree to see Jesus, spoke hypothetically when he said, "*If* I have cheated anybody." One commentator wryly observes, "Past extortion is not in doubt."

5

JEWISH PUPPET GOVERNMENT

Sadducees and Pharisees

Tax collectors were hated by their Jewish countrymen because they were seen as traitors for cooperating with the Romans. They were not, however, entirely alone in this.

There were two groups of religious leaders. The Sadducees were fewer in number but often were from the more prominent families in Jewish society. They were inclined to collaborate with the Romans. As a result, they were shown favor by the Romans, who appointed them to desirable positions. For example, when the Romans interfered in the high priesthood, which had changed from a lifetime to an appointed office, the Romans regularly favored Sadducees. Consequently, many of the priests were Sadducees.

Pharisees, on the other hand, were the nationalistic majority of the populace. They tended to be the scribes and lawyers. As teaching rabbis, they had great influence over the people. Though steeped in Scripture, they mistook the prophecies of a coming Messiah as the promise of a national hero to throw off the hated Roman yoke and restore the glory of David's and Solomon's reigns. For example, they would have encouraged the sentiment that fostered the people's attempt after the feeding of the five thousand to make Jesus their king, by force if necessary.

The Sanhedrin

[The Jewish police] took Jesus to the high priest, and all the chief priests [the Sadducees], elders and teachers of the law [the Pharisees] came together. Peter followed him at a distance, right into the courtyard of the high priest. . . . The chief priests and the whole Sanhedrin were looking for evidence against Jesus so that they could put him to death, but they did not find any. (Mark 14:53-55)

Although they differed widely in their views, the Sadducees and the Pharisees had to work together within the Roman provincial system. The highest Jewish ruling body was a coalition of Sadducees and Pharisees called the Sanhedrin. It was a group of 71 prominent citizens. The main group of 70 is assumed to replicate the 70 elders Moses appointed to help him with his work. The 71st member of the Jewish Sanhedrin was the high priest, the "president" of the group.

The Sanhedrin had almost total control of religious matters in Judea. It also controlled civil and judicial matters as long as they did not encroach on the duties of the procurator (governor). They had a police force, could make arrests on their own, and could even mete out the death sentence. However, they could not carry out an execution without Roman cooperation.

The Mark passage cited previously indicates that on this occasion the Sanhedrin met in the high priest's quarters, but experts debate where their regular meetings were held. Also unknown is how membership to this body was determined.

The low esteem we have of the Sanhedrin is justified by the horrible travesty of justice perpetrated at Jesus' trial. They didn't do much better in Stephen's case either (Acts 7:54-58). But there were also some good men among them. Joseph of Arimathea and Nicodemus were Sanhedrin members. Even before their courageous action on Good Friday (John 19:38,39), Nicodemus lobbied for just treatment of Christ with his challenging question, "Does our law condemn anyone without first hearing him to find out what he is doing?" (John 7:51). Recall also Gamaliel's pragmatic advice that spared the Twelve at their trial before the Sanhedrin (Acts 5:33-40).

Petty Kings

The Jewish nation for all practical purposes fell under Roman rule when in 64 B.C. the Roman general Pompey invaded Syria and Palestine and captured Jerusalem. From then on the Jews were treated as a client state ruled by administrators acceptable to Rome. These administrators bore various titles, but they were petty rulers at best. For a considerable time the descendants of the Maccabees, often referred to as the Hasmonean dynasty, served as independent rulers. But that came to an end when Rome chose to support the rising Herodian dynasty.

In reading the New Testament account, particularly the gospels and Acts, it is occasionally difficult to distinguish which Herod is being spoken of. It is helpful to recognize that the New Testament account covers four generations of Herods.

The Herodians

FIRST GENERATION: HEROD THE GREAT

When Herod realized that he had been outwitted by the Magi, he was furious, and he gave orders to kill all the boys in Bethlehem and its vicinity who were two years old and under, in accordance with the time he had learned from the Magi. (Matthew 2:16)

Herod the Great started out with one major disadvantage for ruling Jewish subjects. He was not Jewish. Rather, he was Idomean (descendent of the Edomites). The Edomites had earlier been conquered by the Jews and forcibly "converted," so they were at best nominally Jewish. But it was not the Jewish people who chose Herod as their ruler. In 47 B.C. the Romans appointed him governor of Galilee at the young age of 25. Herod impressed his Galilean subjects by promptly ridding them of the cave-dwelling bandits infesting their territory, and he impressed the Romans with his efficient tax collecting.

In 37 B.C. the Romans allowed Herod to take the title "king of Judea," but he had to win that position by invading Judea and successfully besieging Jerusalem. Until his death in 4 B.C., he would hold the office of king by terrorizing and tyrannizing his people. (Incidentally, Scripture is clear that Herod died after Jesus was born. His death is now listed as 4 B.C. only because of differences in counting years when the A.D./B.C. system was set up some centuries after Jesus' birth.)

It's hard to call a king "great" when he was so insecure and paranoid that he would kill all the male infants in and around Bethlehem, but that was his mode of operating. On one occasion he had 45 members of the 70-man Sanhedrin executed. False friends and confidants were able to poison his suspicious and fearful mind so that he executed at least three of his sons, as well as his favorite wife, whom he suspected of infidelity. On his deathbed, he ordered that the leading citizens of Jericho be rounded up and locked into the hippodrome, giving strict orders that they be killed when he died so there would be mourning in the city rather than rejoicing over his death.

But there was one area in which Herod can legitimately be called great. He was a great builder. He upgraded Jerusalem to please his Jewish subjects. He built fortresses to protect himself, and he made a trophy city out of Caesarea to honor his Roman overlords.

The building of the temple was surely his major project in Jerusalem, though he also built himself a magnificent palace there and created impressive athletic facilities in the Greek style—this last causing some complaints from the orthodox. The fortress of Masada still stands as an example of his imposing military infrastructure. The totally manmade harbor of Caesarea has been noted previously. The Jewish historian Josephus adds that Herod also constructed a temple to Rome and Augustus, a theater, a hippodrome, an amphitheater, and two large aqueducts to bring water into the city from distant springs.

Herod the Great died unmourned. Two of his political rivals opened the gates of the hippodrome and allowed the imprisoned citizens of Jericho to escape.

SECOND GENERATION: ARCHELAUS, HEROD ANTIPAS, HEROD PHILIP I, HEROD PHILIP II

The second generation of Herods is by all odds the most numerous. That is perhaps not surprising, seeing Herod the Great was successively married to ten different women.

Of the offspring from these marriages, four sons are mentioned in the New Testament:

- Archelaus and Herod Antipas, both sons of Herod the Great's fourth wife, the Samaritan Malthace. These two are the most prominent.

- Herod Philip I, son of Herod the Great's third wife, Mariamne.
- Herod Philip II, son of Herod the Great's fifth wife, a certain Cleopatra of Jerusalem (not the famous Egyptian queen).

Archelaus

In Herod the Great's fifth will, he designated Herod Antipas to succeed him as ruler over Judea. Five days before he died, he added a codicil bestowing that honor on Archelaus. But those five days were too short a time for Rome to ratify the final draft of the will. Predictably, a power struggle developed between the two brothers. While an appeal to Rome for a decision was in progress, there was the threat of an uprising in Jerusalem at the time of the Passover. Archelaus scored points with the Romans by brutally putting down the threat, killing some three thousand Jewish nationalists in the process. Consequently, Rome gave Archelaus control over Judea, Samaria, and Idumea. Herod Antipas, along with his half-brother Herod Philip II, received lesser territorial appointments.

Once established as king, Archelaus ruled with such a heavy hand that the Jews and Samaritans eventually joined in petitioning Rome to remove him from office, which Rome did, exiling him to Gaul (modern France) and replacing him with a Roman governor, Pontius Pilate. Because of Archelaus' brutality, it's no wonder that Joseph and Mary decided to bypass Judea on their return trip after their flight into Egypt. Matthew reports:

> When [Joseph] heard that Archelaus was reigning in Judea in place of his father Herod, he was afraid to go there. Having been warned in a dream, he withdrew to the district of Galilee. (Matthew 2:22)

The lesser appointments referred to previously, given to Herod Antipas and Herod Philip II when Rome handed down its decision regarding Herod the Great's disputed will, were the "tetrarchies" (the term Luke uses in Luke 3). Literally a tetrarch was the ruler over *one-fourth* of a larger territory. It was not a mathematically precise division. Rather, it described an office somewhat lower than a king. Luke carefully places the start of John the Baptist's ministry in the context of the world and local rulers of the day:

> *In the fifteenth year of the reign of Tiberius Caesar—when Pontius Pilate was governor of Judea, Herod [Herod Antipas] tetrarch of Galilee, his brother Philip [Herod Philip II] tetrarch of Iturea and Traconitis, and Lysanias tetrarch of Abilene—during the high priesthood of Annas and Caiaphas, the word of God came to John son of Zechariah in the desert.* (Luke 3:1,2)

Again, the two Herodians in Luke's list are Herod Antipas and Herod Philip II. Together with Lysanias (not part of Herod's family and about whom very little is known) they were the tetrarchs who ruled over three quarters of Palestine. The fourth quarter, consisting basically of Judea and Samaria, had originally been assigned to Archelaus, but after his exile to Gaul, it was administered by Roman governors—Pontius Pilate at the time of John the Baptist and Jesus, as noted.

Herod Philip II

Herod Philip II was the ruler over territory lying north of Galilee. He is mentioned only in Luke chapter 3. (Don't confuse him with the other second-generation Herodion also bearing the name Philip, Herod Philip I, whom we will treat in the following.)

Herod Antipas

Herod Antipas was ruler over Galilee. With his long reign of 43 years (4 B.C.–A.D. 39), Herod Antipas' administration covers all the years of Jesus' life. The first reference to him comes in Luke 3:1, when John the Baptist began his ministry. There are a number of subsequent references to him in the gospels. Three of them have to do with his relationship to Jesus.

> *King Herod heard about this [Jesus' miracles], for Jesus' name had become well known. Some were saying, "John the Baptist has been raised from the dead, and that is why miraculous powers are at work in him."*
> *Others said, "He is Elijah."*
> *And still others claimed, "He is a prophet, like one of the prophets of long ago."*

> But when Herod heard this, he said, "John, the man I beheaded, has been raised from the dead!" (Mark 6:14-16)

This is the Herod who beheaded John the Baptist, and he brazenly admits his heinous crime. Recall how the Pharisees later tried to intimidate Jesus by saying that Herod Antipas was after him also. Luke records:

> At that time some Pharisees came to Jesus and said to him, "Leave this place and go somewhere else. Herod wants to kill you."
>
> He replied, "Go tell that fox, 'I will drive out demons and heal people today and tomorrow, and on the third day I will reach my goal.'" (Luke 13:31,32)

Undaunted, Jesus continued his ministry, which would lead him to Jerusalem where he would, in fact, have a face-to-face encounter with this Galilean ruler, Herod Antipas:

> Pilate asked if the man [Jesus] was a Galilean. When he learned that Jesus was under Herod's jurisdiction, he sent him to Herod, who was also in Jerusalem at that time.
>
> When Herod saw Jesus, he was greatly pleased, because for a long time he had been wanting to see him. From what he had heard about him, he hoped to see him perform some miracle. He plied him with many questions, but Jesus gave him no answer. (Luke 23:6-9)

As far as Jesus' trial was concerned, nothing was accomplished by this meeting. The only result was that Herod Antipas, flattered to be recognized by a Roman overlord, became friends with Pilate.

HEROD PHILIP I

There is yet one more second-generation Herod who makes a cameo appearance in the New Testament record. That is Herod Philip I, son of Herod's third wife, Mariamne. Herod Philip I was not a territorial ruler like the others but was living in Rome as a private citizen. His wife's name was Herodias. Herodias was Mariamne's granddaughter, making her Herod Philip's niece.

On a trip to Rome, Herod Antipas had stopped off to visit his half-brother Herod Philip I. While there he used the occasion to alienate the affection of Herod Philip I's wife, Herodias. Before his return home from Rome, he proposed marriage to Herodias, who used this opportunity to satisfy her political ambitions. (Incidentally, Herodias was also her new husband's niece.) Herodias agreed to marry Herod Antipas on the condition that he divorce the Arabian princess he was married to. Herodias became incensed when John the Baptist disapproved of her new marriage to Herod Antipas, and she eventually secured his death via her equally unscrupulous daughter, Salome, who agreed to ask for John's head on a platter. (Obviously, soap opera is of ancient origin!)

The account is recorded for us by Mark:

Herod [Herod Antipas, ruler of Galilee] himself had given orders to have John arrested, and he had him bound and put in prison. He did this because of Herodias, his brother Philip's [Herod Philip I] wife, whom he had married. For John had been saying to Herod, "It is not lawful for you to have your brother's wife." So Herodias nursed a grudge against John and wanted to kill him. But she was not able to, because Herod feared John and protected him, knowing him to be a righteous and holy man. When Herod heard John, he was greatly puzzled; yet he liked to listen to him.

Finally the opportune time came. On his birthday Herod [Antipas] gave a banquet for his high officials and military commanders and the leading men of Galilee. When the daughter of Herodias came in and danced, she pleased Herod and his dinner guests.

The king said to the girl, "Ask me for anything you want, and I'll give it to you." And he promised her with an oath, "Whatever you ask I will give you, up to half my kingdom."

She went out and said to her mother, "What shall I ask for?"

"The head of John the Baptist," she answered.

At once the girl hurried in to the king with the request: "I want you to give me right now the head of John the Baptist on a platter."

The king was greatly distressed, but because of his oaths and his dinner guests, he did not want to refuse her. So he immediately sent an executioner with orders to bring John's head. The man went, beheaded John in the prison, and brought back his head on a platter. He presented it to the girl, and she gave it to her mother. (Mark 6:17-28)

Third Generation: Herod Agrippa I (A.D. 37–44)

Herodias had a brother, Agrippa, whom historians call Herod Agrippa I. His connection with Herodias immediately prepares one for the worst. H. W. Hoehner writes, "Agrippa I can be considered the black sheep of the Herodian family. He went to school in Rome and lived a careless and extravagant life. . . . He retired quietly to Idumea, leaving many angry creditors behind him in Rome. . . . He repaid old debts by incurring new ones" (*Zondervan Pictorial Encyclopedia of the Bible*, s.v. "Herod").

By currying favor with the Roman emperor Caligula, Herod Agrippa I obtained the tetrarchies ruled by his uncle Herod Philip II and Lysanias. And by maligning his uncle Antipas, he got Antipas banished and subsequently received his holdings in Judea and Samaria. Eventually Herod Agrippa I ruled virtually the same territories as Herod the Great had. This is the Herod we hear about in the book of Acts:

> *It was about this time that King Herod arrested some who belonged to the church, intending to persecute them. He had James, the brother of John, put to death with the sword. When he saw that this pleased the Jews, he proceeded to seize Peter also. This happened during the Feast of Unleavened Bread. After arresting him, he put him in prison, handing him over to be guarded by four squads of four soldiers each. Herod intended to bring him out for public trial after the Passover.* (Acts 12:1-4)

Agrippa I martyred James, the first of the Twelve to die, and intended the same for Peter. No doubt he would have accomplished it too, had an angel not released Peter from his cell. The 16 guards were not so fortunate. Agrippa summarily executed them (Acts 12:19). But the tyrant himself was soon to receive his just reward:

> *Then Herod went from Judea to Caesarea and stayed there a while.*
>
> *On the appointed day Herod, wearing his royal robes, sat on his throne and delivered a public address to the people. They shouted, "This is the voice of a god, not of a man." Immediately, because Herod did not give praise to God, an angel of the Lord struck him down, and he was eaten by worms and died.* (Acts 12:19,21-23)

Fourth Generation: Herod Agrippa II (ca. a.d. 50–100)

Herod Agrippa II was the son of Herod Agrippa I. Because of his youth at the time of his father's early death in A.D. 44, Agrippa II was not immediately raised to power by the Romans. Instead, during Agrippa's early years, Palestine was put under a governor. But gradually the territories of his father were turned over to him.

In a notable understatement, H. W. Hoehner says, "Agrippa II's private life was not exemplary" (*Zondervan Pictorial Encyclopedia of the Bible*, s.v. "Herod"). So constant a companion was he of his widowed sister, Bernice, that there was a persistent rumor of an incestuous relationship between them. Indeed, in the one New Testament appearance Agrippa II makes, the two of them are together. The occasion was when Governor Festus was seeking the help of Agrippa II with the paperwork that needed to accompany Paul's appeal to Caesar:

> *A few days later King Agrippa and Bernice arrived at Caesarea to pay their respects to Festus. Since they were spending many days there, Festus discussed Paul's case with the king. . . .*
>
> *Then Agrippa said to Festus, "I would like to hear this man myself."*
>
> *He replied, "Tomorrow you will hear him."*
>
> *The next day Agrippa and Bernice came with great pomp and entered the audience room with the high ranking officers and the leading men of the city. At the command of Festus, Paul was brought in.*
>
> *[At the conclusion of the hearing] Agrippa said to Festus, "This man could have been set free if he had not appealed to Caesar."* (Acts 25:13,14,22,23; 26:32)

The last words we hear from Agrippa II are words professing Paul's innocence. Secular history records very little about his reign after this point. During the Jewish rebellion (A.D. 70), ending in the destruction of Jerusalem, he protected himself by siding with the Romans. After that, virtually nothing is known of his administration, which is assumed to have lasted until about A.D. 100.

After a run of some 150 years, the Herodian dynasty went out, "not with a bang but a whimper" (T. S. Eliot, "Hollow Men").

6 Christian Interaction with New Testament Society

Orthodox Jewish Community

The Temple

The apostles performed many miraculous signs and wonders among the people. And all the believers used to meet together in Solomon's Colonnade.

Then the high priest and all his associates ... were filled with jealousy. They arrested the apostles and put them in the public jail. But during the night an angel of the Lord opened the doors of the jail and brought them out. "Go, stand in the temple courts," he said, "and tell the people the full message of this new life." (Acts 5:12,17-20)

Although they were not especially welcome, the New Testament Christians continued to use the temple. After all, the New Testament church was born there. The apostles observed daily prayer there, as Peter and John's example attests (Acts 3:1). The Christians regularly assembled there in Solomon's Colonnade. When the Jewish authorities arrested the Twelve, their rescuing angel commanded them to return to the temple and teach. Tradition has it that the apostles continued to serve in Jerusalem for 12 years before heading out to "the ends of the earth." No doubt they continued to work in and around the temple.

The apostle Paul also retained a high regard for the temple. Although his missionary journeys started from Antioch on the Orontes, they always ended with a return to Jerusalem and the temple. His continuing attachment to the temple is particularly evident at the close of the third missionary journey.

When we arrived at Jerusalem, the brothers received us warmly. The next day Paul and the rest of us went to see James, and all the elders were present. (Acts 21:17,18)

There was a problem in Jerusalem. Paul's teaching of salvation as a pure gift, without the addition of any law works, was misunderstood—as though Paul was forbidding people to follow Old Testament customs even if, in Christian freedom, they chose to continue using them. The Jerusalem leadership's suggested solution strongly involved the temple.

> *So do what we tell you. There are four men with us who have made a vow. Take these men, join in their purification rites and pay their expenses, so that they can have their heads shaved. Then everybody will know there is no truth in these reports about you, but that you yourself are living in obedience to the law.* (Acts 21:23,24)

Paul agreed to take part in the purification rites in the temple and to pay for the sacrifices needed to fulfill a vow that four men had taken. Paul's actions did not compromise grace but were rather an indication of his continuing attachment to God's house. Christians were, after all, the true heirs of the temple.

THE SYNAGOGUE

The temple was basically a *public* worship center; the local synagogue was not. It was a rather closed community. The local synagogue was the heart and core of every Jewish community. It was their church, their school, their library, their social center, the relief agency, and the judge and jury in disputed matters. For Christians to lose that support connection was a serious blow.

One indication of the loss Christians suffered when put out of the synagogues is the major relief effort that was needed to administer the "daily distribution of food" to widows in Jerusalem (Acts 6). When this relief work overwhelmed the apostles, seven deacons were appointed to handle the work. Previously, these widows had likely been served by their synagogues. Recall also the major collection Paul organized among Gentile Christians to support the needy saints in Jerusalem, a need no doubt increased by the loss of local synagogue help.

Jesus had earlier warned his followers:

> *"You must be on your guard. You will be handed over to the local councils and flogged in the synagogues."* (Mark 13:9)

Not only were the synagogues no longer helpful to individual Christians, but they proved decidedly hostile to the Christian message. Time and again Paul was driven out by opposition coming from the synagogue. And yet, synagogues made one major contribution to the Christian cause.

> Then [Paul and Barnabas] returned to Lystra, Iconium and Antioch, strengthening the disciples and encouraging them to remain true to the faith. . . . Paul and Barnabas appointed elders for them in each church and, with prayer and fasting, committed them to the Lord, in whom they had put their trust. (Acts 14:21-23)

How could Paul, after a stay of only a few weeks or months, put these young congregations on their own? The answer seems to lie with the synagogue background of the "elders" whom the apostles put in charge. Synagogue worshipers have rightly been called People of the Book. Devoted to the reading and study of the Old Testament, the synagogue immersed its members in the Old Testament Scripture with its messianic promises. Those who accepted Paul's message that Jesus of Nazareth was that promised Messiah very quickly became mature Christians. They were well equipped to serve congregations by sharing that message with their fellow Jews and with their Gentile neighbors, who had very little knowledge of God's saving message as outlined in the Old Testament. Unwittingly, the synagogue thus became "the cradle" of the Christian church.

Interaction With Roman Government: Christianity as a "Legal Religion"

> While Gallio was proconsul of Achaia, the Jews made a united attack on Paul and brought him into court. "This man," they charged, "is persuading the people to worship God in ways contrary to the law."
>
> Just as Paul was about to speak, Gallio said to the Jews, "If you Jews were making a complaint about some misdemeanor or serious crime, it would be reasonable for me to listen to you. But since it involves questions about words and names and your own law—settle the matter yourselves. I will not be a judge of such things." So he had them ejected from the court. (Acts 18:12-16)

As noted previously, the Roman government usually allowed conquered people to keep their national religion, thus making it a legal religion. Judaism was such a legal religion. In an interesting exchange in the city of Corinth, this religious legality was extended to include Christianity.

As if concerned about Roman laws, the local Jews accused Paul and the Christians of worshiping illegally. Gallio, the governor over the province of Achaia (Greece), didn't see it that way. To him the disagreement about Jesus of Nazareth being the promised Messiah was a mere internal quibble, a question "about words and names and [their] own law." Gallio didn't have a clue as to how important that distinction was, but God used him for his own purpose. In his uninformed state, Gallio threw the case out of court, thereby lumping Christianity with Judaism and making it equally legitimate. This decision gave Paul an extended "window" for working in Corinth. Luke tells us his work there lasted a year and a half, the second-longest stay recorded in Acts.

Emperor Worship

Generally speaking, the Romans tolerated the recognized legal religions—but not always. When Paul in Corinth joined up with the Jewish tent-making couple of Aquila and Priscilla, Luke tells us they were natives of Pontus (Black Sea area) "who had recently come from Italy . . . because Claudius [A.D. 41–54] had ordered all the Jews to leave Rome" (Acts 18:2).

Christians too were persecuted at times. There were crucifixions under the mad emperor Nero (A.D. 54–68), who was trying to deflect blame from himself for a disastrous fire in Rome. But these persecutions of Jews and Christians were sporadic and mostly confined to Italy.

However, with the arrival of emperor worship, sustained persecutions over wide regions began.

> *I, John, your brother and companion in the suffering and kingdom and patient endurance that are ours in Jesus, was on the island of Patmos because of the word of God and the testimony of Jesus.* (Revelation 1:9)

Deification of leaders was not a new idea in the Mediterranean world. The Greeks had their "heroes," supposedly descended from the gods. For centuries the Egyptians had been worshiping their pharaohs. Even in Palestine, recall Herod Agrippa's willingness to accept divine honors (Acts 12:22,23).

Also in Rome there was an impulse to deify popular leaders, but initially that occurred only after a ruler's death. For example, Julius Caesar was deified after his assassination. His successor was Octavian, whom the senate gave the honorific title of "Augustus." However, promoting the fiction that he was merely *princeps* ("first citizen"), Augustus did not allow himself to be called god.

The push for deifying emperors didn't initially come from Rome but from the provinces. The city of Pergamum, on mainland Asia Minor next to the island of Patmos where John was exiled, was the first to dedicate a temple to the goddess Rome and her leaders. The provinces of Galatia and Bithynia soon followed suit; Egypt and Spain did likewise.

It was no doubt a tribute to Rome's skill in incorporating territories that conquered provinces became loyal and patriotic subjects. But there was also a self-serving aspect to emperor worship: it curried favor with the emperors, who were all too susceptible to flattery. Toward the end of the first century, they were not only willing to accept divine honors but so egotistical that Emperor Domitian (A.D. 81–96) demanded to be addressed as *Dominus et Deus,* "Lord and God."

For most pagans, it was no problem to add another deity to their pantheon of gods. For monotheistic Christians, it was an unthinkable compromise. When challenged by the authorities, they could save themselves by cursing Christ or even by merely offering a pinch of incense at the emperor's altar. Refusing to do so, however, made them look perverse or unpatriotic—in either case, enemies of the state and subject to persecution.

Revelation names only one martyr, Antipas in Pergamum (2:13), but John is in exile at the time of Domitian and is addressing brothers in suffering. Things would get even worse after the turn of the century, but as history has often shown, the blood of the martyrs is the seed of the church. During the time of Constantine (A.D. 312), Christianity became the official religion of the empire.

BIBLIOGRAPHY

Davis Dictionary of the Bible. Grand Rapids: Baker Book House, 1956.
The Oxford Classical Dictionary. London: Oxford University Press, 1964.
Zondervan Pictorial Encyclopedia of the Bible. Grand Rapids: Zondervan, 1976.

Index

A

academy, 42, 43
agricultural illustrations of Jesus, 8, 9
agricultural society, 7–9
amphiblestron, 25–29
angling, 22–24
Appleby, John F., 14
Aquila and Priscilla, 48
Archelaus, 123–125
architecture of synagogue, 42
artisans, 45–49
Assembly, House of, 41
Augustus, 92, 93, 117, 118

B

Babylonian captivity, 39, 40
barbel, 30, 31
bartering, 50–53
Battle of Actium, 91
Battle of Pharsalus, 90
Battle of Philippi, 91
Brutus and Cassius, 90, 91

C

Caesar Augustus, 92, 93, 117, 118
Carmelite Monks of Wyoming, 64, 65
carpenters, 46, 47
cart method of threshing, 17, 18
casting net, 25–29
census, Roman, 117, 118
centurions, 103–106
Chinnereth, Lake, 70–73
Christian church, early, 12, 13
Christianity as legal religion, 132, 133
citizenship, Roman, 115–118
coasting, 74–77
codex, 35, 36

coin in fish's mouth, 23, 24, 31
coins, 51–53
   large sums of, 53–55
   nationality of, 56, 57
   small sums of, 55, 56
   value-neutral, 56–61
commanders, 99–103
communication through roads, 69, 70
constitution of Roman Republic, 85–89
construction trades, 45–49
consul, 85–87, 89
Cornelius, 104–106
craftsmen, 45–49

D

daric, 51
Dead Sea Scrolls, 39
deification, 134
denarius, 52–54, 57
diet of New Testament people, 22
diktyon, 27–29
drachma, 52, 58
dragnet, 24, 25, 28, 29

E

early Christian church, 12, 13
education, 41–43
Egnatian Highway, 67
emperor worship, 133, 134
Ezra, 33

F

farming, 7–9
feeding of over five thousand, 29, 30
Felix, 110–112
Fertile Crescent, 67

fig trees, 18–20
First Triumvirate, 89, 90
fish, 29–32
fish symbol, 32
fish, coin in mouth of, 23, 24, 31
fishing, 22–29
four kinds of soil, 7–9
freighter, 76, 78, 80

G

Gaius Marius, 89, 90
Galilee, Sea of, 70–73
Gamaliel, 42–44
gemstones, 60, 61
Genneserat, Lake, 70–73
Gentiles, 11–13, 105, 106
governors, 97–99, 111, 112
grafting, 12, 13
grain harvesting, 14–18
grapevines, 9–11
Great Rift Valley, 71
guidelines for scribes, 33, 34

H

handwritten manuscripts, 32–36
harvest parables, 14–16
harvesting, 14–18
Hasmonean dynasty, 121, 122
Herod Agrippa II, 129
Herod Antipas, 123–128
Herod Philip I, 124, 126, 127
Herod Philip II, 124, 125
Herod the Great, 110, 122–124
Herodian Agrippa, 114
Herodians, 122–129
Herodias, 127, 128
Hillel, 43
homeschooling, 39, 41, 42
hook-and-line fishing, 22–24
House of Assembly, 41
House of Prayer, 41
House of Study, 41

I

ichthus, 32
Ides of March, 90
Irenaeus, 70

J

Jerusalem, 7
Jesus
  as carpenter, 46, 47
  as environmentalist, 31, 32
  invites disciples to follow him, 25, 26
  prayer life of, 72, 73
  as teacher, 44, 45
Jewish community, 130–132
John the Baptist, 18, 127
Josephus, 47, 48, 59, 123
Julius Caesar, 89, 90
Julius, centurion, 107–109

K

King's Highway, 67

L

Lake Chinnereth, 70–73
Lake Genneserat, 70–73
lawyers, 36–39
legal religion, Christianity as, 132, 133
legal system of Rome, 109–115
lepta, 55, 56
local leadership under Rome, 115, 118
Lucius Sulla, 89, 90

M

Maccabees, 121, 122
Marc Antony, 90, 91
Marcus Crassus, 90
Marcus Lepidus, 90, 91
Martyr, Justin, 47

McCormick, Cyrus, 14
Mediterranean climate, 7–9
military of Rome, 100–109
mina, 52, 54
miracles of Jesus
   catches of fish, 27–29
   coin in fish's mouth, 23, 24, 31
   feeding of over five thousand, 29, 30
   fig tree, 20
monarchy of Rome, 84, 85
money changers, 58
money loans, 59
mounts, 66
mustard plants, 21, 22

N

Nero, 133
netting fish, 24–29
new Jerusalem, 60
nomadic people, 48

O

ocean travel, 73–82
Octavian, 90–92
olive trees, 12, 13
oral tradition, 38

P

Palestine, 7, 8
   occupied by Rome, 93, 94
papyrus, 34–36
parables of Jesus
   harvest, 14–16
   mustard seed, 21, 22
   shrewd manager, 50, 51
   sower, 8, 9
   talents, 59
   tenants, 10, 11
   weeds and the wheat, 14–16
   workers in the vineyard, 52, 53

parchment, 34–36
Pax Romana, 93, 111
pearls, 60
persecution, 133
Pharisees, 37, 38, 120, 121
Phoenicians, 73, 77
Pompey the Great, 90, 93, 94
Pontius Pilate, 95, 98, 124, 125
Porcius Festus, 112–115, 129
port-hopping, 74–77
Prayer, House of, 41
prayer life of Jesus, 72, 73
proconsuls, 95–97
procurators, 97–99, 111, 112
provinces of Rome, 94–109
publishing, 32–36

Q

quill pen, 35
quorum, 40

R

rains, 7, 8, 15
relationship of Gentiles to Jews, 12, 13
Remus, 83, 84
Republic of Rome, 85–91
requirements for scribes, 33, 34
roads, 66–70
Roman
   census, 117, 118
   citizenship, 115–118
   Empire, 91–93
   legal system, 109–115
   military, 100–109
   monarchy, 84, 85
   occupation of Palestine, 93, 94
   provinces, 94–109
   Republic, 85–91
   roads, 67–70
   social classes, 85–89
   taxes, 118, 119

INDEX

Rome, founding of, 83, 84
Romulus, 83, 84, 101
rowboat, 71

S

Sadducees, 120, 121
sagene, 24, 25, 28, 29
Saint Peter's fish, 23, 24, 31
Sanhedrin, 120, 121
sardines, 30
scribes, 33–39
scriptorium, 36
scrolls, 35
Sea of Galilee, 70–73
Sea of Tiberias, 70–73
Second Triumvirate, 90, 91
Shamai, 43
ships, 73
shipwreck, 81, 82, 109
shul, 41
sledge method of threshing, 17, 18
social classes of Roman Republic, 85–89
soils, 7–9
Solomon's navy, 70
stadion, 72
stater, 57, 58
stonecutters, 47, 48
Study, House of, 41
stylus, 35
symbol of fish, 32
synagogue, 39–42, 131, 132

T

talents (coins), 52, 54, 55
taxes, 23, 24, 57, 58, 118, 119
teachers of the law, 36–39
teaching, 39–45
Tel Aviv, University of, 11, 26, 61
temple, 47, 130, 131
temple taxes, 23, 24, 57, 58

tent making, 48, 49
threshing, 15–18
throw net, 25–29
tilapia, 31
Torah, 33, 37, 40
trampling method of threshing, 17
travel
    distances, 66, 67
    on foot, 62–65
    Levitical regulation for, 20
    necessities, 63–65
    by ocean, 73–82
    by riding, 65, 66
    routes, 66–70
    by water, 70–82
Triumvirate, First and Second, 89–91
Tyrian shipping, 73, 74

U

University of Tel Aviv, 11, 26, 61

V

Via Egnatia, 67
Via Maris, 67
vineyards, 10, 11

W

water travel, 70–82
Way of the Sea, 67
weeds, 14–16
weights and measures, 50, 51
wheat, 14–16
widow's offering, 55, 56
wine's roles and features, 9–11
winepresses, 10, 11
winnowing, 18
Wisconsin Lutheran Seminary, 11, 26, 61
writing materials, 34–36